HARCOURT
SOCiAL Studies

Communities
Around Our World

Harcourt
SCHOOL PUBLISHERS

www.harcourtschool.com

HARCOURT SOCIAL Studies

Communities Around Our World

Series Authors

Dr. Michael J. Berson
Professor
Social Science Education
University of South Florida
Tampa, Florida

Dr. Tyrone C. Howard
Associate Professor
UCLA Graduate School of Education
& Information Studies
University of California Los Angeles
Los Angeles, California

Dr. Cinthia Salinas
Assistant Professor
Department of Curriculum and
Instruction
College of Education
The University of Texas at Austin
Austin, Texas

North Carolina Consultants and Reviewers

Jenny Bajorek
Teacher
Northwoods Elementary School
Cary, North Carolina

Dan Barber
Teacher
Idlewild Elementary School
Charlotte, North Carolina

Brianne Beck
Teacher
Allen Jay Elementary School
High Point, North Carolina

Melissa Blush
Teacher
Allen Jay Elementary School
High Point, North Carolina

Ardelia Brown
Teacher
Pearsontown Elementary School
Durham, North Carolina

Alice M. Cook
Teacher
Paw Creek Elementary School
Charlotte, North Carolina

Lori D. Davis
Teacher
C. Wayne Collier Elementary School
Hope Mills, North Carolina

John D. Ellington
Former Director
Division of Social Studies
North Carolina Department of Public
Instruction
Raleigh, North Carolina

Laura Griffin
Teacher
Sherwood Park Elementary School
Fayetteville, North Carolina

Sharon Hale
Teacher
Hillandale Elementary School
Durham, North Carolina

Dr. Ted Scott Henson
Educational Consultant
Burlington, North Carolina

Charlotte Heyliger
Teacher
C. Wayne Collier Elementary School
Hope Mills, North Carolina

Tony Iannone
Teacher
Nathaniel Alexander Elementary School
Charlotte, North Carolina

Judith McCray Jones
Educational Consultant
Former Elementary School
Administrator
Greensboro, North Carolina

Gwendolyn C. Manning
Teacher
Gibsonville Elementary School
Gibsonville, North Carolina

Courtney McFaull
Teacher
Sherwood Park Elementary School
Fayetteville, North Carolina

Lydia Ogletree O'Rear
Teacher
Elmhurst Elementary School
Greenville, North Carolina

Marsha Rumley
Teacher
Brooks Global Studies
Greensboro, North Carolina

Dean P. Sauls
Teacher
Wayne County Public Schools
Goldsboro, North Carolina

Melissa Turnage
Teacher
Meadow Lane Elementary School
Goldsboro, North Carolina

Joseph E. Webb
Educational Consultant
Adjunct Professor
East Carolina University
Greenville, North Carolina

Harcourt
SCHOOL PUBLISHERS

ISBN-13: 978-0-15-356636-3
ISBN-10: 0-15-356636-1

6 7 8 9 10 11 12   1678   17 16 15 14 13 12
4500343523

Unit 1

Meeting People

Ben's Room

Unit 2

Good Citizenship

Changing People and Places

Special Days

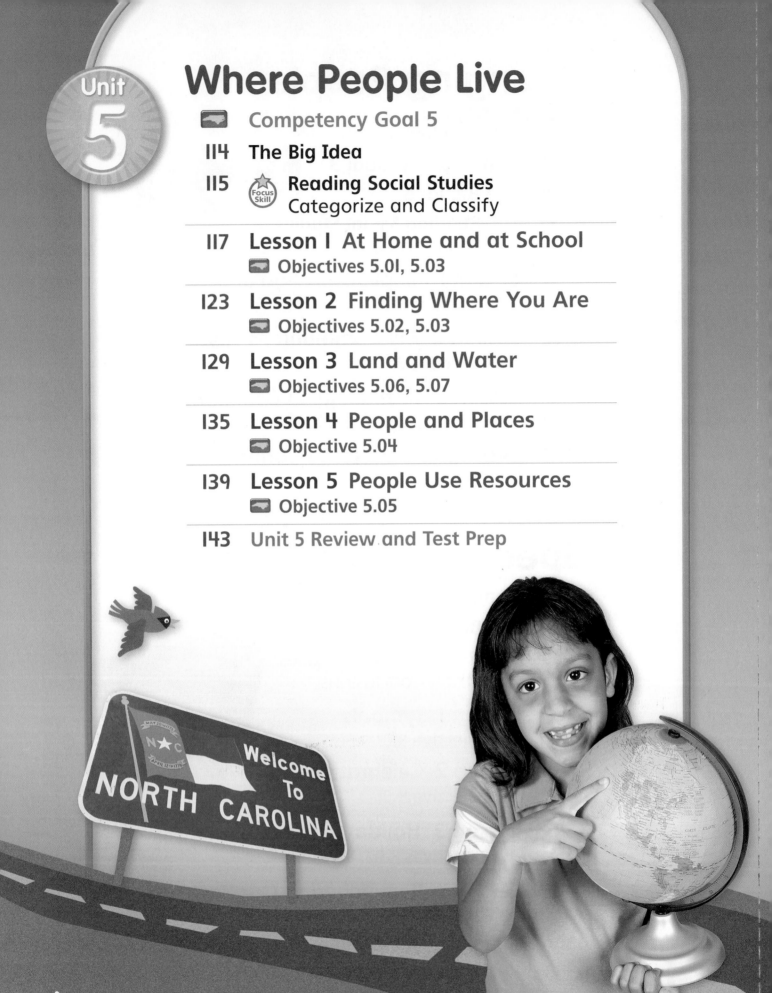

Unit 5

Where People Live

Competency Goal 5

Welcome To NORTH CAROLINA

Unit 7

Technology We Use Today

Competency Goal 7

Geography Review

The Five Themes of Geography

The story of people is also the story of where they live. When scientists talk about Earth, they think about five themes, or main ideas.

Location

Everything on Earth has its own location.

Place

Every place has features that make it different from other places.

GEOGRAPHY

Human-Environment Interactions

People can change the environment or change their ways to live in it.

Movement

People, goods, and ideas move every day.

THEMES

Regions

Areas of Earth have features that make them different from other areas.

Looking at Earth

The shape of Earth is shown best by a globe. A **globe** is a model of Earth.

On a map of the world, you can see all the land and water at once. A **map** is a flat drawing that shows where places are.

Much of the world is covered by large bodies of water called **oceans**.

A **continent** is one of seven main land areas on Earth.

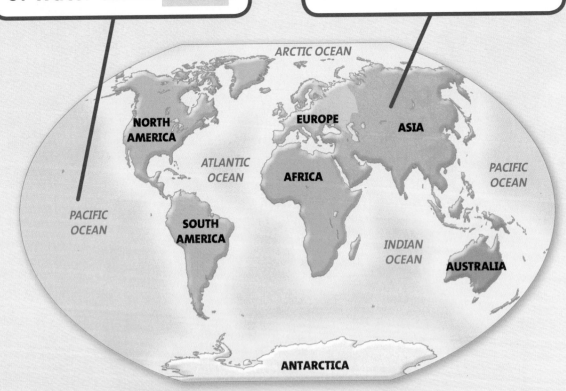

ARCTIC OCEAN

NORTH AMERICA

EUROPE

ASIA

ATLANTIC OCEAN

AFRICA

PACIFIC OCEAN

PACIFIC OCEAN

SOUTH AMERICA

INDIAN OCEAN

AUSTRALIA

ANTARCTICA

Name the seven continents and four oceans you see on the map.

Your Address

You live on the continent of North America in a **country** called the United States. Your address names the **city** and **state** in which you live.

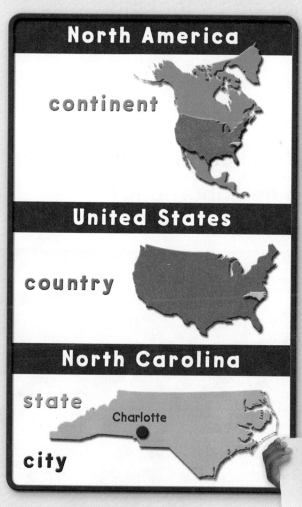

North America
continent

United States
country

North Carolina
state
Charlotte
city

Mari Tyler
123 Pine Street
Charlotte, N.C. 28269

What is your address?

View from Above

Does your neighborhood have a school, a grocery store, a library, a fire station, a park, and a bank? These are places that people share in a neighborhood. You can learn about a neighborhood by looking at a photograph.

How does a photograph taken from above help you study a neighborhood?

You can also learn about a neighborhood by looking at a map. Mapmakers draw symbols to help you find places on the map. A **map symbol** is a small picture or shape that stands for a real thing. The **map title** tells you what the map shows.

How is this map like the photograph? How is it different?

Neighborhood Map

Reading Maps

Maps are used to show many different kinds of information. This is a map of the United States. On this map, you can use the map key to find our national capital, or our country's capital. You can also use the key to find each state's capital and borders. A **border** is a line that shows where a state or country ends.

Locate the state of North Carolina on the map. What is the state capital? Name the states that border North Carolina.

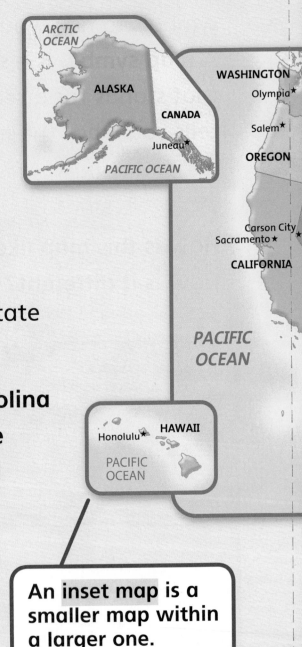

An **inset map** is a smaller map within a larger one.

Check the map title to see what area is being shown.

The United States

CANADA

MONTANA
★Helena

NORTH DAKOTA
★Bismarck

MINNESOTA

Lake Superior

NEW HAMPSHIRE
VERMONT

MAINE
★Augusta

IDAHO
★Boise

SOUTH DAKOTA
★Pierre

St. Paul

MICHIGAN

Lake Huron

Montpelier★

NEW YORK
Albany★

Lake Ontario

★Concord
Boston
★MASSACHUSETTS
★Providence

WYOMING

WISCONSIN
Madison
★

Lake Michigan

Lansing
★

Lake Erie

Hartford★

RHODE ISLAND
CONNECTICUT

NEVADA

Cheyenne★

IOWA

Des Moines
★

PENNSYLVANIA

★Trenton

★Salt Lake City

NEBRASKA

OHIO
Columbus
★

Harrisburg★

NEW JERSEY
★Dover

Denver★

Lincoln★

INDIANA

Annapolis★

DELAWARE

UTAH

COLORADO

Topeka
★

Jefferson City★

Springfield
★

Indianapolis
★

WEST VIRGINIA

⊛
Washington, D.C.
MARYLAND

KANSAS

MISSOURI

Charleston
★

Frankfort
★

★Richmond

ARIZONA

OKLAHOMA

KENTUCKY

VIRGINIA

Santa Fe
★

Oklahoma City
★

ARKANSAS

TENNESSEE

★Nashville

Raleigh★NORTH CAROLINA

Phoenix
★

NEW MEXICO

Little Rock★

ALABAMA

★Atlanta

Columbia
★

SOUTH CAROLINA

ATLANTIC OCEAN

MISSISSIPPI

GEORGIA

TEXAS

LOUISIANA

Jackson
★

Montgomery
★

Austin
★

Baton Rouge
★

★Tallahassee

FLORIDA

MEXICO

North

West ✦ East

South

Gulf of Mexico

A **compass rose** shows directions. The **cardinal directions** are north, south, east, and west.

Map Key
⊛ National capital
★ State capital
— Border

The **map key** shows what the symbols on the map mean. Symbols may be pictures, colors, patterns, lines, or other special marks.

Geography Terms

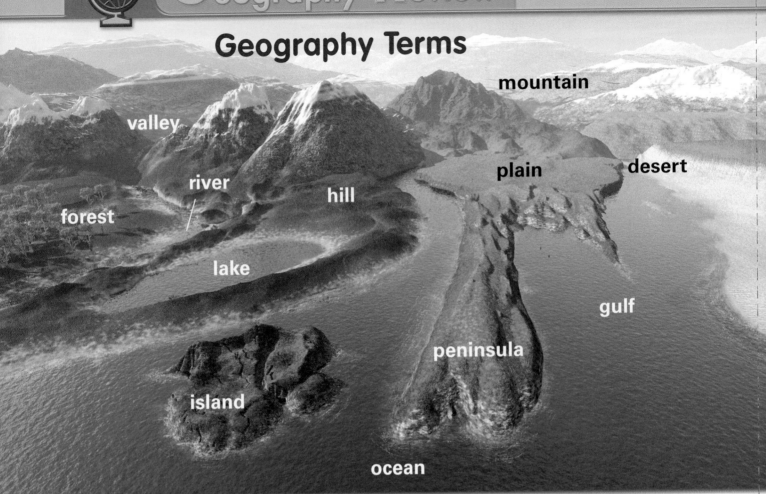

desert a large, dry area of land

forest a large area of land covered with trees

gulf a large body of ocean water that is partly surrounded by land

hill a landform that rises above the land around it

island land with water all around it

lake a body of water with land all around it

mountain the highest kind of landform

ocean a body of salt water that covers a large area

peninsula land that is surrounded on only three sides by water

plain flat land

river a large stream of water that flows across the land

valley low land between hills or mountains

Meeting People

Children play a game together.

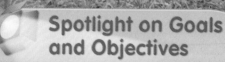

Spotlight on Goals and Objectives

North Carolina Interactive Presentations

NORTH CAROLINA STANDARD COURSE OF STUDY

COMPETENCY GOAL 1 The learner will analyze how individuals, families, and groups are similar and different.

 # The Big Idea

How are people, families, and groups the same? How are they different?

There are many kinds of groups of people. A group is a number of people who do things together. A group can be as big as all the people in a community. A group can be as small as a family. Even though people belong to different groups, the groups are the same in many ways.

Draw a picture of a group you belong to.

Focus Skill Compare and Contrast

Learn

■ You compare two things by thinking about how they are the same.

■ You contrast two things by thinking about how they are different.

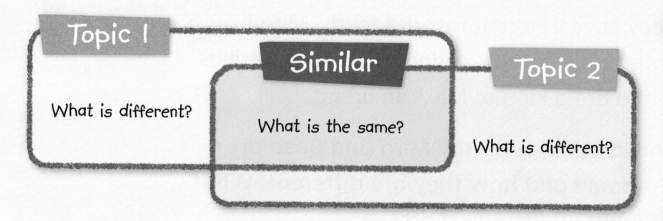

Topic 1

What is different?

Similar

What is the same?

Topic 2

What is different?

Practice

Read the paragraph below. Underline the sentence that tells how Ian and Jack are the same.

Ian and Jack both belong to the book club. Ian also belongs to the cooking club. Jack belongs to the art club.

Topic 1
Topic 2

Apply

Read the paragraphs.

Mira and Rosa are best friends. They live in Greenville, North Carolina. Mira's family is from Poland. She speaks Polish and English. Rosa's family is from Mexico. She speaks Spanish and English.

Mira and Rosa both like to play basketball. They have different favorite foods. Mira likes a Polish soup called chlodnik. Rosa likes tortillas, which are a kind of Mexican bread.

This chart shows how Mira and Rosa are the same and how they are different. What can you add to the chart?

Mira

Her family is from Poland.

_____

_____

Similar

They live in Greenville, North Carolina.

_____

_____

Rosa

Her family is from Mexico.

_____

_____

4

Roles in a Family

A **family** is a group of people who live together. People in a family share things. We **share** when we use something with others. Families also work and play together. What will you learn about families?

_____

_____

A family enjoys a park in North Carolina.

NORTH CAROLINA STANDARD COURSE OF STUDY

1.01 Describe the roles of individuals in the family.

5

The Roles of Parents

TextWork

❶ Underline one sentence that tells about a parent's role in the family.

There are many kinds of families. A family may be big or small. Each person in a family has a role. A **role** is the part a person plays in a group.

Parents work at jobs to earn money. They use this money to buy things for their families. Parents also take care of their children.

The Roles of Children

Children have many roles in their families. Most children help around the house. They may wash the dishes, make their beds, or set the table. Older children may help care for their younger brothers and sisters.

TextWork

② Look at the pictures. Circle the jobs children can do.

7

1 **SUMMARIZE** What roles do people play in a family?

_____

_____

_____

2 What is a **family**?

_____

_____

3 How is a child's role in a family different from a parent's role?

_____

_____

_____

Writing

✏️ Write two sentences about your roles in your family.

Many Groups

My name is Macy. I belong to many groups. I am a part of my family, my class, my school, and other groups. **What might you learn about groups?**

_____

_____

**NORTH CAROLINA
STANDARD COURSE OF STUDY**

1.02 Identify various groups to which individuals and families belong.

9

Groups I Belong To

I am a daughter in my family. I set the table for dinner.

I am in first grade. I water our class plants.

I am a soccer goalie. I keep the other team from scoring.

I am in an art club. I make sure there are brushes for everyone.

10

Groups My Family Belongs To

My family is part of many groups. We belong to the **community** where we live and work.

We go to the community center. We are in the swim club.

We are also part of a larger family group. We have aunts, uncles, cousins, and grandparents.

 **TextWork**

2 Underline the sentences that name groups Macy's family belongs to.

1 **SUMMARIZE** What kinds of groups do people and families belong to?

_____

_____

_____

2 What are some groups in your **community**?

_____

_____

_____

3 What groups does Macy belong to?

_____

_____

_____

Activity

Think about the groups you belong to. Draw pictures to show these groups.

Families Are the Same and Different

In many ways, people and families are the same. They can be different, too. Ben has just moved to a new city. He is learning about the people there. **What will you learn about people and families?**

_____

_____

Ben's Room

NORTH CAROLINA STANDARD COURSE OF STUDY

1.03 Compare and contrast similarities and differences among individuals and families.

13

Different Cultures

TextWork

❶ Name one thing that is part of a group's culture.

_____

Ben likes learning about the cultures in his new city. A **culture** is a group's way of life. Things such as food and clothing are parts of a group's culture.

Ben has also learned about different customs. **Customs** are ways of doing things. The children in his new school come from different cultures. Their families have different customs.

Sharing Traditions

A **tradition** is something that is passed on from older family members to children. Ben's family makes a sweet bread on special days. Hailey's family has a special quilt. Learning about different cultures, customs, and traditions helps people get along.

Biography

Caring

John Coltrane

John Coltrane was a jazz musician from North Carolina. He played the saxophone and recorded many songs. He used music from different cultures. He spent his life sharing their different musical traditions.

1 **SUMMARIZE** How are families the same? How are they different?

_____

_____

_____

2 Why do the children in Ben's school have different **customs**?

_____

_____

3 Why is it important to learn about different cultures, customs, and traditions?

_____

_____

_____

Writing

Write about a tradition you share with your family members.

We Live in the United States

4

People have come from around the world to live in the United States. The **world** is all the people and places on Earth. People from other places make the United States interesting. **What will you learn about people from different places?**

_____

_____

The Statue of Liberty in New York Harbor

**NORTH CAROLINA
STANDARD COURSE OF STUDY**

1.04 Explore the benefits of diversity in the United States.

17

❶ Underline the sentence that tells you what an immigrant is.

Immigrants in the United States

Kweli, Anahat, Yana, and Juan are making a scrapbook. They are immigrants to the United States. An **immigrant** is a person who comes from another place to live in a country.

Kweli is from Kenya. Kweli's family sells African art.

Anahat is from India. Anahat's family owns an Indian restaurant.

Families who come to the United States bring their cultures. They share their cultures with others. Immigrants have brought many new customs to our country.

People of different cultures live and work together. This makes the United States an interesting place.

❷ How are Yana's family and Juan's family alike?

_____

_____

Yana's mother teaches ballet, which she learned in Russia.

Juan's grandmother sells cloth that she learned to make in El Salvador.

Lesson 4 Review

1 **SUMMARIZE** How have people from different countries made the United States more interesting?

_____

_____

2 Where do **immigrants** come from?

_____

_____

3 How are Anahat, Kweli, Juan, and Yana like you?

_____

How are they different from you?

_____

_____

Activity

What countries did people in your family live in before they came to the United States? Mark the places on a map.

Review and Test Prep

 The Big Idea

People come from different places. They may also belong to different groups. They still share many things.

Summarize the Unit

Focus Skill **Compare and Contrast** Fill in the chart. Show what you have learned about the roles of children and the roles of parents.

Children

go to school

_____

_____

_____

_____

Similar

_____

_____

_____

_____

_____

Parents

_____

_____

_____

_____

Use Vocabulary

Fill in the blanks with the correct words.

Word Bank

family
 p. 5
share
 p. 5
community
 p. 11
customs
 p. 14
world
 p. 17

1 A group of people who live together

is called a _____.

2 Most families are part of a larger

_____ made up of other

families.

3 People have come from all over the

_____ to live in the United States.

4 People in a family _____ with one

another.

5 Some people may have special

_____, or ways of doing things.

Think About It

Circle the letter of the correct answer.

6 Which is a role that a child would have?

A going to school

B buying food

C going to work

D driving a car

7 Which is a part of a group's culture?

A the playground

B computers

C clothing

D television

8 Which is a kind of tradition?

A making a special food

B reading a book

C going to school

D playing outside

9 Which is a person who comes from another place to live in a country?

A a role

B a group

C a culture

D an immigrant

Answer each question in a complete sentence.

10 Why do you think traditions are important to families?

_____

_____

_____

11 Why do you think immigrants come to the United States?

_____

_____

Show What You Know

Writing Write a Paragraph
Think about your culture and another culture. Write about how they are the same and different.

Activity Plan a Culture Fair
Find out about a culture in your community. Make a booth with activities and displays. Hold the culture fair.

GO online To play a game that reviews the unit, join Eco in the North Carolina Adventures online or on CD.

Good Citizenship

Students take turns voting in a class election.

Spotlight on Goals and Objectives

North Carolina Interactive Presentations

NORTH CAROLINA STANDARD COURSE OF STUDY

COMPETENCY GOAL 2 The learner will identify and exhibit qualities of good citizenship in the classroom, school, and other social environments.

 # The Big Idea

How do people show they are good citizens?

A citizen lives in and belongs to a community. We follow rules at home, at school, and in our community. When we do this, we are being good citizens. Good citizens also help others in their community.

Draw a picture that shows a child being a good citizen.

Focus Skill Main Idea and Details

Learn

■ The main idea tells you what you are reading about. It is the most important idea.

■ A detail gives more information. The details explain the main idea.

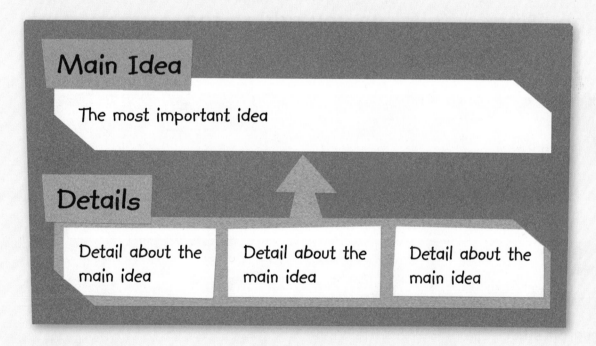

Main Idea

The most important idea

Details

| Detail about the main idea | Detail about the main idea | Detail about the main idea |

Practice

Read the paragraph below. Underline one of the sentences that tells a detail.

There are many kinds of rules. We follow rules at home. We follow rules at school. We follow rules in our community.

Main Idea

Detail

27

Apply

Read the paragraph.

Anna follows rules at home for helping her family. She puts her things away and keeps her room clean. She reads to her little brother. Anna also sets the table before dinner.

The chart below shows the main idea of the paragraph. What details can you add to the chart?

Main Idea

Anna follows rules at home for helping her family.

Details

| Anna puts her things away and keeps her room clean. | _____ _____ _____ | _____ _____ _____ |

Rules and Laws

A person who lives in and belongs to a community is a **citizen**. Citizens must follow the rules of their community. A **rule** tells people how to act. We follow rules when we work and play.

What might you learn about rules?

_____

_____

All dogs must be on leash. Clean up after your dogs.

NORTH CAROLINA STANDARD COURSE OF STUDY

2.04 Recognize the need for rules in different settings.

Rules at School

TextWork

❶ Circle the reasons we have rules at school.

❷ Draw and write a class rule. Add it to the bulletin board.

At school, rules help us learn and get along. Rules also help us stay safe.

We have different rules for different parts of the school. When we walk in the hall, we have to be quiet. When we play outside, we do not have to be quiet.

Work quietly.

Be kind.

Rules in a Community

Communities have rules called laws. A **law** is a rule that people in a community must follow.

Communities have many kinds of laws. Laws are important for citizens in a community. They tell people how to live together safely. They also help keep communities clean.

 **TextWork**

3 Circle the sign that tells where people might be crossing the street.

1 SUMMARIZE Why do we need rules and laws?

_____

_____

_____

2 What is a **citizen**? Use your own words to tell.

_____

_____

_____

3 What are some rules that your class follows?

_____

_____

_____

Activity

Draw a picture that shows someone following a law.

Leaders

A **leader** is a person who works to help a group. There are many kinds of leaders. Leaders make sure people follow rules and laws. **What might you learn about leaders?**

_____

_____

A coach is the leader of a team.

NORTH CAROLINA
STANDARD COURSE OF STUDY

2.02 Identify the roles of leaders in the home, school, and community such as parents, mayor, police officers, principal, and teacher.

Leaders in the Community

✏️ **TextWork**

❶ Circle the names of the people who are leaders at school.

❷ Name one kind of leader in a community.

_____

Parents are leaders at home. They make rules to keep children safe.

Teachers are leaders at school. Our teacher helps make the class rules.

A **principal** leads the whole school. Our principal works with parents and teachers to make our school safe.

Police Station

Teacher

Principal

Police Officer

A **mayor** is the leader of a community. Our mayor works to make our community a good place to live.

Communities have other leaders, too. Police officers make sure that people follow the laws. Firefighters help when there is a fire.

Mayor William Bell of Durham, North Carolina, with citizens

Firefighter

Librarian

Mayor

Lesson 2 Review

1 **SUMMARIZE** How do leaders help people?

_____

_____

_____

2 What is the job of a **principal**?

_____

_____

_____

3 Who are some leaders in a community?

_____

_____

_____

Writing

Write a sentence that tells about a leader in your community.

36

Following the Rules

Rules and laws help us be fair. Being **fair** means acting in a way that is right for all. Sometimes people do not follow rules. This causes problems for everyone. **What do you think you will learn about following rules?**

_____

_____

**NORTH CAROLINA
STANDARD COURSE OF STUDY**

2.05 Identify the need for fairness in rules by individuals and by people in authority.

2.06 Predict consequences that may result from responsible and irresponsible actions.

37

Playing Fairly

It is important to be fair when you do things with others. When you play games fairly, everyone can have fun. If you do not play fairly, other children may not want to play with you.

Consequences

People who break laws face consequences. A **consequence** is something that happens because of what a person does or does not do.

Consequences can be bad or good. Children who break a rule might have to miss something that is fun. Children who follow rules might get more playtime.

 **TextWork**

2 What can happen if you break a rule?

_____

_____

People who cross a street at the wrong place may get hurt.

39

1 SUMMARIZE Why is it important for people to follow rules and laws?

_____

_____

_____

2 What does it mean to be fair?

_____

_____

_____

3 What are some consequences of breaking a rule?

_____

_____

_____

Activity

Act out some ways of playing fairly.

Being a Good Citizen

Citizens of the United States have rights. A **right** is something people are free to do. People also have responsibilities. A **responsibility** is something you should do. **What do you think you will learn about being a good citizen?**

_____

_____

Volunteers help Habitat for Humanity build houses for people.

NORTH CAROLINA STANDARD COURSE OF STUDY

2.01 Develop and exhibit citizenship traits in the classroom, school, and other social environments.

Rights

People in the United States have many rights. They also have many freedoms. A **freedom** is a kind of right.

TextWork

❶ Circle the person who is using the right of freedom of speech.

Freedom of the press is the right to write about ideas in newspapers.

Freedom of assembly is the right to meet in groups.

Freedom of speech is the right to speak about our ideas.

Good Citizens

Good citizens are responsible. You are being responsible when you do the things you should do.

One way to be responsible is to help others. A **volunteer** works without pay to help people. Another way is to show respect for people and things. To show **respect** is to treat someone or something well.

❷ What is one of your responsibilities at school?

_____

_____

I am responsible for . . .

caring for my community.

learning in school.

cleaning up my room.

43

1 SUMMARIZE How can you be a good citizen?

_____

_____

_____

2 What is one **right** that you have?

_____

_____

_____

3 How can you show respect for others?

_____

_____

_____

Writing

Make a list of some of your responsibilities.

Make a Choice by Voting

When you **vote**, you make a choice that gets counted. Americans vote for many leaders in our government. A **government** is a group of people who make the laws. **What do you think you will read about voting?**

_____

_____

People wait in line for their turn to vote.

**NORTH CAROLINA
STANDARD COURSE OF STUDY**

2.03 Participate in democratic decision-making.

45

How to Vote

You can use a ballot to vote. A **ballot** shows all the choices. A ballot can be on paper. It can also be on a voting machine.

You mark your choice on a ballot. The choice that gets the most votes wins.

TextWork

❶ What do you use a ballot for?

_____

Biography

Citizenship

Elizabeth Dole

Elizabeth Dole is a United States senator. She is from Salisbury, North Carolina. She has worked with six United States Presidents. She was also the President of the American Red Cross. The Red Cross helps people when bad things such as floods happen.

Vote for Class Leaders

Mrs. Johnson's class used ballots to vote for a class leader. The choices were Marc, Tami, and Carlos.

2 Look at the chart that counts the votes. Circle the name of the person who will be the class leader.

Votes

Marc				
Tami	##		
Carlos	#### ####

☆ **BALLOT** ☆

Mrs. Johnson's Class
To VOTE, connect the head and tail of the arrow pointing to your choice, like this:

Vote for ONE Class Leader

Marc ←

Tami ←

Carlos ←

1 **SUMMARIZE** How can you make a choice that gets counted?

_____

_____

_____

2 What does a **government** do?

_____

_____

3 What are two kinds of ballots?

_____

_____

_____

Activity

List games your class would like to play. Have each person vote. Count the votes. Which game will you play?

Review and Test Prep

 The Big Idea

It is important to be a good citizen in your community. Good citizens help others. They also vote for their community leaders.

Summarize the Unit

Focus Skill **Main Idea and Details** Fill in the chart. Show what you have learned about voting.

Main Idea

Good citizens vote for leaders in their community.

Details

They use a ballot to vote.

Use Vocabulary

Fill in the blanks with the correct words.

Word Bank

citizen
p. 29

law
p. 31

leader
p. 33

vote
p. 45

government
p. 45

When I grow up, I will ❶ _____

in elections. By voting, I will help choose the

people who run our community. This group

of people, called a ❷ _____,

helps everyone get along. I am a good

❸ _____ in my community.

I follow every ❹ _____,

or rule. One day, I want to be a

❺ _____ in my community.

Think About It

Circle the letter of the correct answer.

6 Which is the leader of a school?

    A the principal

    B the government

    C a teacher

    D the mayor

7 Which does a leader help a community do?

    A read books

    B plant trees

    C make laws

    D make food

8 What is respect?

    A to speak about ideas

    B to treat someone or something well

    C to write about ideas

    D to belong to groups

9 Which shows all of the choices you can vote for?

    A a teacher

    B a government

    C a ballot

    D a freedom

Answer each question in a complete sentence.

⑩ Who are some leaders in your community?

_____

_____

⑪ What are some freedoms that Americans have?

_____

_____

⑫ What happens when people break laws?

_____

_____

Show What You Know

Writing Write a List
Imagine that a new child has joined your class. Write a list of class rules to help the new child.

Activity Plan a Campaign Rally
Choose two people to run for Class Safety Monitor. Make posters and signs. Tell about safety rules at the rally.

GO online To play a game that reviews the unit, join Eco in the North Carolina Adventures online or on CD.

Changing People and Places

A family looks at pictures from long ago in a scrapbook.

 The Big Idea

How do people and places change?

To change is to become different. The ways people dress, work, and play can change over time. Some places change, too. People may build new roads and buildings. Some changes, such as changing clothes, happen every day. Some changes, such as growing up, happen over a long time.

Draw a picture of how you have changed over a long time.

Reading Social Studies

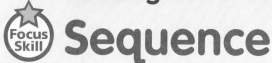

Sequence

Learn

■ Sequence is the order in which things happen. What happens first? What happens next? What happens last?

■ Look for sequence words such as <u>first</u>, <u>next</u>, <u>then</u>, <u>later</u>, <u>last</u>, and <u>finally</u>.

First — What happens first → Next — What happens next → Last — What happens last

Practice

Read the paragraph below. Underline the sentence that tells what happens after Justin puts the letter into an envelope.

Justin wrote a letter to his grandmother. He needs to mail it to her. First, Justin puts his letter into an envelope. Next, he puts a stamp on the envelope. Last, Justin puts his letter into the mailbox.

Sequence

Apply

Read the paragraph.

Long ago in North Carolina, the school day was not like your school day. All the grades shared one classroom. First, they all read out loud. Next, each grade was called up for a lesson while the other children worked quietly. Last, the children helped the teacher do chores. They cleaned the classroom and got wood for the fire.

This chart shows the order in which things happened on a school day long ago. What can you add to the chart?

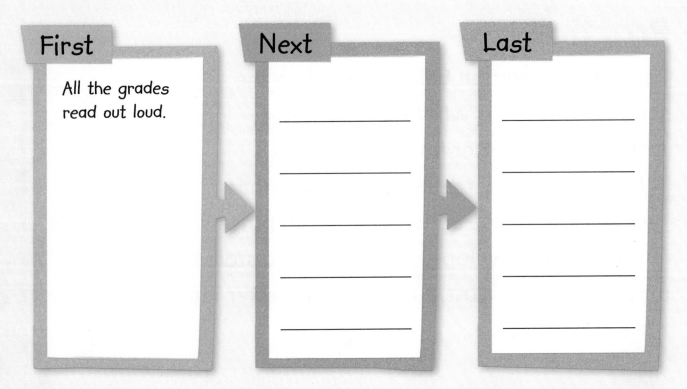

First

All the grades read out loud.

Next

_____

_____

_____

_____

_____

Last

_____

_____

_____

_____

People Long Ago and Today

Grandma Mary tells Darla about when she was a child. Grandma Mary was a child in the **past**, the time before now. Darla is a child in the **present**, the time now. **What do you think you will learn about the past and the present?**

_____

_____

A school in Wayne County, North Carolina, from the past

**NORTH CAROLINA
STANDARD COURSE OF STUDY**

3.01 Describe personal and family changes, past and present.

57

Clothes in the Past

TextWork

❶ Underline the clothes Grandma Mary wore when she was a little girl.

❷ Circle the clothes that Darla likes to wear.

Darla watches old home movies with Grandma Mary. The movies show how people dressed in the past. "I always wore dresses when I was a little girl," Grandma Mary says.

Darla has dresses, but she likes to wear jeans and T-shirts. The clothes people wear change over time. To **change** means to become different.

Families Past and Present

Grandma Mary tells Darla about her family. "Like many other women in the past, my mother worked at home. She took care of my brothers and me."

Today, both men and women work at home. Men and women also have jobs outside the home.

3 Underline the sentence that tells where Grandma Mary's mother worked.

Family Life

🖊 **TextWork**

❹ Underline some of the ways families change.

Families change in the present just as they did in the past. Children grow into adults. People get married. Families move.

Grandma Mary tells Darla about the fun she had as a little girl. "Every year, we went to see the Azalea Festival. The festival is in Wilmington, North Carolina," she says. "People still go to it today."

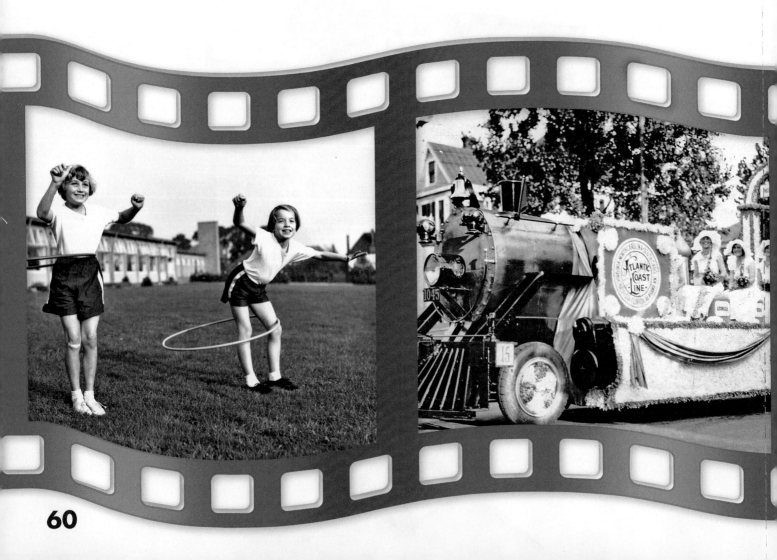

Communication

Every day, people talk and write to share ideas and feelings. This sharing is called **communication**.

Long ago, Grandma Mary wrote letters to her friends. She also talked to them on the telephone. Today, Darla and Grandma Mary still communicate in these same ways. They also send letters and pictures by e-mail.

❶ SUMMARIZE How is the way you live different from the way people lived long ago?

_____

_____

_____

❷ Write a sentence that tells about **communication** between two people.

_____

_____

❸ What is one thing Grandma Mary did for fun as a little girl?

_____

_____

_____

Writing

✎ Write sentences about what you think it would have been like to live in the past.

My Community's History

Lily's class is learning about her community. Every community has a history. **History** is the story of what happened in the past. Lily will learn how her community has changed. **What might you learn about your community?**

_____

_____

Lily visits different places in her community, Durham, North Carolina.

NORTH CAROLINA STANDARD COURSE OF STUDY

3.02 Describe past and present changes within the local community.

63

Learning About the Past

TextWork

1 Underline the places you can visit to learn about your community's history.

Lily visits some places in her community to learn about its history. She visits the library. She also visits the history museum. People at these places tell Lily about her community's history.

Lily goes to the library in Durham.

A Changing Community

Lily finds books and photographs at the library. She also talks to older people in the community. They talk to her about her community's past. She also learns about her community's present.

Lily will use what she has learned to write about her community. You can learn and write about your community, too.

TextWork

2 What is one thing you can find at a library?

_____

Lily talks to her grandparents.

Lesson 2 Review

① SUMMARIZE Why do you think it is important to know about your community's past and present?

_____

_____

② How might you learn about the **history** of your community?

_____

_____

③ What are some of the ways Lily finds out about her community's past?

_____

_____

Activity

Draw a picture to show what your community might have looked like in the past.

Technology in Communities

Technology is the tools we use to make our lives easier. A **tool** is something that people use to do work. Over time, changes in technology bring changes to communities. What will you learn about how technology has changed?

_____

_____

Statesville, North Carolina

**NORTH CAROLINA
STANDARD COURSE OF STUDY**

3.02 Describe past and present changes within the local community.

3.04 Recognize that members of the community are affected by changes in the community that occur over time.

Changes in Home Tools

![TextWork icon] **TextWork**

❶ Circle the picture of the tool that looks most like a tool people use today.

Homes are filled with tools. Some of these are toasters, washers, and dryers. People are always making new tools. Tools make work easier. Over time, new and better tools are made.

Clothespins, an iron, and a washer from long ago

Children in History

George S. Parker

George S. Parker was good at thinking up new games. In 1883, when he was 16 years old, he sold his first game. He and his brothers started a company. They made many of the board games that we play today.

Schools
Long Ago and Today

Schools have changed over time. Long ago, schools had only one room and one teacher. Children of all ages learned together.

Today, schools have many rooms and many teachers. Some ways of learning are the same as in schools long ago. Some ways are different.

 **TextWork**

2 Circle something in the picture of the classroom of long ago that is also in your classroom.

One-room school, 1917

School Tools

Long Ago	Today
A B C	

Transportation
Long Ago and Today

Transportation is ways of moving people and things from place to place. In the past, transportation was very slow. Many people never went far from where they were born.

Technology has changed this. Boats, trains, cars, and planes are safer and faster. Today, people can travel far away—even into space!

70

Jobs Long Ago and Today

New technology has changed the ways people work. Some jobs are no longer needed. Workers no longer take milk and ice to people's homes. Grocery stores now have refrigerators and freezers.

New technology has also made new jobs. Workers now use robots to make some things. A robot is a machine that can do a job.

TextWork

4 What is one kind of job that is no longer needed because of new technology?

_____

_____

The way people tell the news has changed.

Long Ago

Today

1 **SUMMARIZE** How has technology changed the way people live in communities?

_____

_____

_____

2 Give examples of different kinds of **transportation**.

_____

_____

3 Why do we no longer need workers to deliver milk and ice to homes?

_____

_____

Writing

✏ Write sentences about a tool we use today that makes our lives easier.

Changes in Communities

Marc and Antonio are pen pals. They live in different countries. A **country** is a land with its own people and laws. The two boys share how their communities have changed. **What might you learn about how places change?**

_____

_____

Marc lives in Asheville, North Carolina.

**NORTH CAROLINA
STANDARD COURSE OF STUDY**

3.03 Compare and contrast past and present changes within the local community and communities around the world.

① What is one thing people in Asheville did long ago that they still do today?

_____

_____

Changes in Marc's Community

Long ago, families started to move to Asheville, North Carolina. They built homes, schools, and stores. The town grew.

Soon the railroad came to Asheville. People worked to help build it. They also began to build and work in hotels. Today, people in Asheville still work in hotels. They also make things such as chairs and tables.

Asheville, Long Ago

Asheville, Today

Changes in Antonio's Community

Antonio liked learning about Asheville. Now he wants to tell Marc how Rome has changed.

Rome is a very old city in Italy. New buildings have been built. Old buildings have been made to look new on the inside. Other buildings have been made to look as they did in the past.

TextWork

2 Circle something that is the same in both pictures of Rome.

Rome, Long Ago

Rome, Today

75

③ What other communities has Marc learned about?

_____

_____

_____

Communities Around the World

Marc and Antonio want to learn about other communities around the world. Marc made a web page about the communities he has learned about. It tells how they have changed over time. Antonio plans to add more communities to the web page.

marcswebpage.com\li-ming

Li Ming

Li Ming lives in Harbin. Harbin is an old city in China. People built a railroad there. Harbin became very large!

marcswebpage.com\ayi

Ayi

Ayi lives in Accra. It is near the ocean in Ghana. People sailed there from many countries. They shared their cultures.

4 How is Li Ming's community like Tia's community?

_____

_____

marcswebpage.com\tia

Tia

Tia lives in Cuzco, Peru. Cuzco is an old city. People go there to learn about the Inca, who lived there long ago.

Lesson 4 Review

1 **SUMMARIZE** How are today's communities like the communities of long ago?

_____

_____

2 Write a sentence about a **country** you have learned about in this lesson.

_____

_____

3 Many years ago, people began moving to Marc's community, Asheville. What happened to Asheville after people moved there?

_____

_____

Activity

Make a booklet about one of the communities in this lesson. Tell how that community has changed over time.

Review and Test Prep

 The Big Idea

The ways people live change over time. Some places change, too. Some places stay the same.

Summarize the Unit

Focus Skill **Sequence** Fill in the chart. Show what you have learned about how transportation has changed.

First	Next	Last
Transportation was very slow long ago. Many people did not travel far from home.	_____ _____ _____ _____ _____ _____ _____	_____ _____ _____ _____ _____ _____

Use Vocabulary

Fill in the blanks with the correct words.

Zack's class is learning about the

1 _____ of his community.

Zack has learned how people lived in the

2 _____, or the time before

now. He knows how people live now, in the

3 _____. Zack learned how things

4 _____, or become different. One

way is that people now use cars instead of horses.

Cars are one kind of **5** _____ that

makes our lives easier.

Word Bank

past
  p. 57

present
  p. 57

change
  p. 58

history
  p. 63

technology
  p. 67

Think About It

Circle the letter of the correct answer.

6 Which sentence tells about life long ago?

- **A** People lived in communities.
- **B** People went to space.
- **C** People used e-mail.
- **D** People used cell phones.

7 What is a country?

- **A** an ocean
- **B** a land with its own people and laws
- **C** a mountain
- **D** a valley

8 Which has made transportation safer and faster?

- **A** communication
- **B** e-mail
- **C** robots
- **D** technology

9 How did people communicate in the past?

- **A** They used cell phones.
- **B** They wrote letters.
- **C** They sent e-mails.
- **D** They drove cars.

Answer each question in a complete sentence.

10 How has communication changed over time?

_____

_____

11 What are some ways you can learn about how your community has changed?

_____

_____

Show What You Know

Writing Write a Story
All things change. People change, too. Think about when you were younger. Write a story about a memory from that time.

Activity Make a Scrapbook
Make a scrapbook about your community's past and present. Draw or cut and paste pictures of life in the past and present on the pages. Then share your scrapbook.

GO online To play a game that reviews the unit, join Eco in the North Carolina Adventures online or on CD.

Special Days

A band plays at the Yam Festival in Tabor City, North Carolina.

Spotlight on Goals and Objectives

North Carolina Interactive Presentations

NORTH CAROLINA STANDARD COURSE OF STUDY

COMPETENCY GOAL 4 The learner will explain different celebrated holidays and special days in communities.

83

The Big Idea

How do we remember special days and people?

A special day is a time to be happy about something that is important to you. Americans and people all over the world have many special days. On these days, we remember special times and people.

Draw a picture of a day that is special to you.

Focus Skill # Draw Conclusions

Learn

- A conclusion is something you figure out from facts in what you are reading.

- Think about what you already know. Remember the new facts you learn.

- Combine new facts with the facts you already know to draw a conclusion.

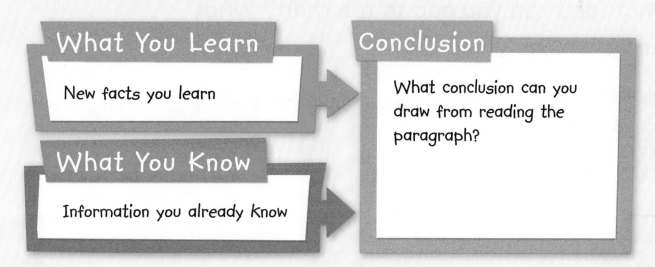

What You Learn

New facts you learn

What You Know

Information you already know

Conclusion

What conclusion can you draw from reading the paragraph?

Practice

Read the paragraph below. Underline the sentence that draws a conclusion.

Our flag is a symbol of the United States. We stand when we pledge allegiance to the flag. We honor the United States flag.

Fact

85

Apply

Read the paragraph.

Luke lives in Southport, North Carolina. He is getting ready to go to a Fourth of July celebration with his family. There will be a parade in the afternoon and fireworks at night. Luke makes sure to wear red, white, and blue. He practices singing patriotic songs. Luke takes an American flag with him.

What facts can you add to the chart? What conclusion can you draw?

What You Learn

Luke wears red, white, and blue.

_____

_____

What You Know

Red, white, and blue are the colors of the United States.

Conclusion

_____

_____

_____

_____

_____

_____

A **symbol** is a picture that stands for an idea or a thing. The American flag is a symbol for the United States. A **flag** is a piece of cloth with symbols on it. **What will you learn about symbols?**

_____

_____

These children show respect for the flag by saying the Pledge of Allegiance.

**NORTH CAROLINA
STANDARD COURSE OF STUDY**

4.01 Recognize and describe religious and secular symbols/celebrations associated with special days of diverse cultures.

American Symbols

TextWork

❶ Underline the symbols of the United States.

The United States has many symbols. These symbols stand for ideas. These ideas are important to us.

Some symbols are plants. Some are animals. The rose and the bald eagle are American symbols.

The Liberty Bell stands for freedom.

The bald eagle is our national bird.

The pictures on our money are symbols, too.

North Carolina Symbols

North Carolina has symbols, too. Some symbols are plants. Some are animals that live in North Carolina. The gray squirrel is the state animal. The box turtle is also a North Carolina symbol.

North Carolina has a flag. The colors and shapes on the flag are symbols, too.

TextWork

2 What are the dates shown on the flag?

_____

_____

State Flag

Gray Squirrel

Box Turtle

Lesson 1 Review

1 **SUMMARIZE** Why are the symbols for our country and state important?

_____

_____

_____

2 Where have you seen our country's **flag**?

_____

_____

3 What do you think would be a good symbol for your community? Why?

_____

_____

_____

Activity

Draw a flag for your class. Put symbols on it for things that are important to your class.

Celebrations

A **celebration** is a time to be happy about something special. Some celebrations are just for family and friends. A **holiday** is a day of celebration for everyone. **What might you learn about celebrations?**

_____

_____

Dancers at the Folkmoot International Festival in Waynesville, North Carolina

NORTH CAROLINA STANDARD COURSE OF STUDY

4.01 Recognize and describe religious and secular symbols/celebrations associated with special days of diverse cultures.

Holidays of Religion

TextWork

1 Underline the meaning of <u>religion</u>.

2 Circle something special that people do on each holiday of a religion.

On some holidays, people celebrate something in their religion. A **religion** is a set of beliefs about God or gods. Families eat special foods and do special things on these days.

Christmas

At Christmas, some Christian families put up Christmas trees. They celebrate the birthday of Jesus.

Hanukkah

At Hanukkah, Jewish families light candles on a menorah. Hanukkah is celebrated for eight nights.

Ramadan

At Ramadan, Muslims eat only at night for one month. They visit with family and friends.

Vesak

At Vesak, Buddhists remember the life of Buddha. They have parades to honor him.

Holi

At Holi, Hindus celebrate the coming of spring. They wear bright colors. They even throw colored water on each other!

Celebrations of Culture

✏️ **TextWork**

3 Circle the picture that shows Chinese New Year.

When people move to the United States, they still celebrate holidays from their culture. Celebrations help us learn about each other.

Irish Americans celebrate St. Patrick's Day with parades. They eat Irish foods.

The Chinese New Year lasts for 15 days. It ends with a Lantern Festival.

TextWork

4 Underline the names of the celebrations of culture.

At Kwanzaa, African Americans celebrate their culture. People learn about very old African ideas.

Mexican Americans celebrate Cinco de Mayo. This is a day to honor Mexico.

The Cherry Blossom Festival is in Washington, D.C. It celebrates the city's cherry trees. These trees were a gift from Japan.

1 **SUMMARIZE** Why do people celebrate holidays?

_____

_____

_____

2 What is one **holiday** your community celebrates?

_____

_____

_____

3 Why do people in the United States celebrate holidays from different cultures?

_____

_____

_____

Writing

✏️ Write about a holiday that you learned about in this lesson.

Holidays and Heroes

A **national holiday** is a day to remember an event that is important to our country. It may also remember a hero. A **hero** is a person who does something to help others. **What kinds of holidays might you read about?**

_____

_____

NORTH CAROLINA
STANDARD COURSE OF STUDY

4.02 Explore and cite reasons for observing special days that recognize celebrated individuals of diverse cultures.

4.03 Recognize and describe the historical events associated with national holidays.

Remembering Heroes

TextWork

❶ Circle the picture of the person who was once President of the United States.

Our country has many heroes. We have holidays to remember them.

Dr. Martin Luther King, Jr., Day honors Dr. King. He helped all Americans have the same rights.

Presidents' Day was once a holiday to remember our first President. His name was George Washington. Now it is a day to remember all of our Presidents.

Orville and Wilbur Wright flew the first airplane with a motor. On December 17, we remember the work they did.

Cesar Chavez made sure farmers were treated fairly. We remember him on March 31.

2 Who worked so that all people could have the right to vote?

_____

Susan B. Anthony believed that all people should have the right to vote. The work she did helped make this happen. We remember her on February 15.

Memorial Day and Veterans Day are two national holidays. On these days, we remember those who have helped in our country's wars.

Honoring History

Some holidays help us remember important days in our country. To do this, we learn about history. For example, we learn about the Pilgrims. Long ago, the Pilgrims showed their thanks for a good harvest. They shared a dinner with the Wampanoag. The Wampanoag are American Indians. American Indians were the first people to live in North America.

TextWork

3 Circle the food many Americans eat on Thanksgiving Day.

turkey

pizza

We remember the dinner of the Wampanoag and the Pilgrims. We call this holiday Thanksgiving.

TextWork

4 Circle the picture that shows Americans celebrating our country's birthday.

July 4 is Independence Day. It is our country's birthday. On this day, we celebrate our country's freedom. Many communities have parades and fireworks.

On Constitution Day, we remember the day when our country's first leaders signed the United States Constitution.

101

Lesson 3 Review

1 **SUMMARIZE** Why do we have national holidays?

_____

_____

_____

2 Name a person you think is a **hero**. Tell why you think he or she is a hero.

_____

_____

3 Our country's birthday is July 4. What do we celebrate on this day?

_____

_____

_____

Activity

With your class, make a calendar showing our country's national holidays.

Remembering Our Past

We know that it is important to remember the past. People have different ways of remembering the past. Some people visit landmarks. A **landmark** is a symbol that is a place people can visit. **What might you learn about the history of a community?**

_____

_____

Bodie Island Lighthouse in North Carolina

**NORTH CAROLINA
STANDARD COURSE OF STUDY**

4.04 Trace the historical foundations of traditions of various neighborhoods and communities.

103

American Indians

American Indians helped new settlers. A **settler** is a person who makes a home in a new community. American Indians showed the settlers how to grow food. They grew corn and potatoes.

Biography

Sacagawea

Sacagawea was a Shoshone Indian. As a young woman, Sacagawea met Meriwether Lewis and William Clark. They wanted to go through the western part of North America. Sacagawea said that she would be their guide. She helped them in many ways.

Today, many American Indians live in North Carolina. One of these groups is the Cherokee. There is a city in North Carolina called Cherokee.

There is a special landmark in Mount Gilead, North Carolina. It is called the Town Creek Indian Mound. Here, people can learn how American Indians lived long ago.

Cherokee Doll

TOWN CREEK INDIAN MOUND

3 Look at the picture. What does it show about Latin American culture?

_____

_____

The Latin American Festival

The Latin American Festival is held each year in Charlotte, North Carolina. It celebrates Latin American culture and history.

The Latin American Festival has music and dancing. There is Latin American art. There is also food from Latin American culture.

Latin American Dancers

Highland Games

Highland Games celebrate Scottish culture and history. The Foothills Highland Games and Festival takes place every year in Hendersonville, North Carolina. At the Foothills Highland Games and Festival, people eat Scottish food and play Scottish games. They also wear special Scottish clothes and dance to Scottish music.

TextWork

4 What culture do people celebrate at the Foothills Highland Games and Festival?

_____

Scottish Bagpipe Players

1 SUMMARIZE Why do you think people celebrate their culture from long ago?

_____

_____

2 Tell about a **landmark** in your state.

_____

_____

_____

3 What are some of the ways people take part in the Latin American festival?

_____

_____

_____

Writing

Write sentences about the ways different communities in North Carolina remember their past.

Review and Test Prep

 The Big Idea

On holidays, we remember special events and people.

Summarize the Unit

Focus Skill **Draw Conclusions** Fill in the chart.

Show what you know about celebrations.

What You Learn

Bobby invited his friends to a party. They all played games and ate cake.

Conclusion

_____

_____

_____

_____

_____

_____

_____

_____

_____

What You Know

We remember special days with celebrations.

Use Vocabulary

Write the word under its meaning.

① a day to remember a person or an event that is important to our country

_____

② a person who does something to help others

_____

③ a set of beliefs about God or gods

_____

④ a piece of cloth with colors and shapes that stand for things

_____

⑤ a symbol that is a place people can visit

_____

> **Word Bank**
>
> **flag**
>   p. 87
> **religion**
>   p. 92
> **national holiday**
>   p. 97
> **hero**
>   p. 97
> **landmark**
>   p. 103

Think About It

Circle the letter of the correct answer.

6 Which is a symbol of North Carolina?

    A the rose

    B the bald eagle

    C the blue wolf

    D the gray squirrel

7 Which holiday honors Mexico?

    A Cinco de Mayo

    B St. Patrick's Day

    C the Cherry Blossom Festival

    D Chinese New Year

8 Which is a national holiday?

    A Vesak

    B Kwanzaa

    C Independence Day

    D Holi

9 Which of these symbols is a landmark?

    A flag

    B Town Creek Indian Mound

    C rose

    D bald eagle

Answer each question in a complete sentence.

⑩ What are some holidays that celebrate a religion?

_____

_____

⑪ Why do we celebrate national holidays?

_____

_____

⑫ What does a settler do?

_____

_____

Show What You Know

Writing Write a Poem
Think about a famous symbol or landmark. Why is it a good symbol or landmark? Write a poem about it.

Activity Plan a Patriotic Party
Plan to celebrate an American hero, holiday, symbol, or landmark. Make invitations and classroom decorations.

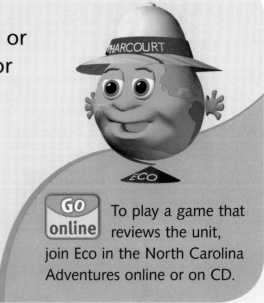

GO online To play a game that reviews the unit, join Eco in the North Carolina Adventures online or on CD.

Where People Live

A family walks on the beach in Bald Head Island, North Carolina.

Spotlight on Goals and Objectives

North Carolina Interactive Presentations

NORTH CAROLINA STANDARD COURSE OF STUDY

COMPETENCY GOAL 5 The learner will express geographic concepts in real life situations.

The Big Idea

How do people use maps and globes to tell about places?

People live in many different places. Some people live near water. Other people live on hills. We can tell about where we live by using maps and globes. We can also use these tools to find out about new places.

Draw a picture of the place where you live.

Categorize and Classify

Learn

■ When you categorize and classify, you sort things into groups.

■ Decide what each group will be called.

■ Place each thing in a group.

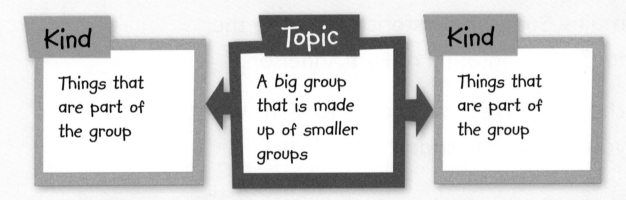

Kind

Things that are part of the group

Topic

A big group that is made up of smaller groups

Kind

Things that are part of the group

Practice

Read the paragraph below. Underline the category of places you go to shop. Then circle the places that can be classified as places to shop.

There are many different places in your community. There are places you go to learn, like schools and libraries. There are places you go to shop, like malls and grocery stores.

Categorize

Classify

115

Apply

Read the paragraphs.

North Carolina has many places to visit. People go to cities like Raleigh and Charlotte. Families visit fun places like the North Carolina Zoo and the Jungle Rapids Family Fun Park.

Other people visit national parks such as the Blue Ridge Parkway or the Great Smoky Mountains. Some visit historic places like the Alamance Battleground or Fort Anderson.

The chart below shows places to visit. What can you add to the chart?

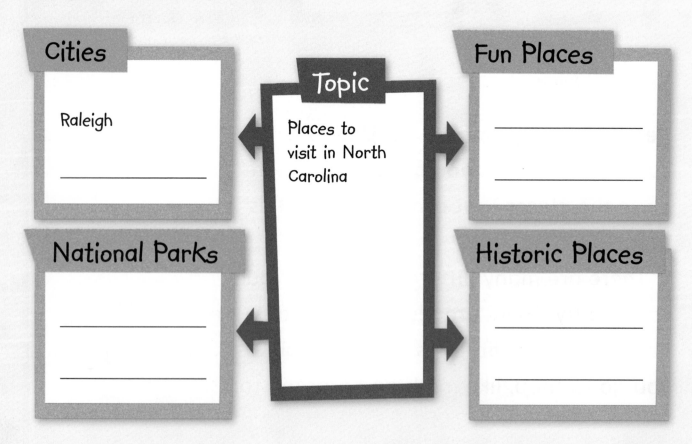

Cities

Raleigh

_____

Topic

Places to visit in North Carolina

Fun Places

_____

_____

National Parks

_____

_____

Historic Places

_____

_____

Maps show **location**, or where places are. Maps can show small places, such as parks. Maps can also show large places, such as communities. **What do you think you will learn about maps?**

_____

_____

Many people visit the North Carolina Zoo, in Asheboro.

NORTH CAROLINA STANDARD COURSE OF STUDY

5.01 Locate and describe familiar places in the home, classroom, and school.

5.03 Use geographic terminology and tools to create representations of the earth's physical and human features through simple maps, models, and pictures.

At Home

You can use maps to show where things are in your home. Tim knows where to find things in his home. He drew a map of the inside of his home. The map shows the location of each room.

TextWork

❶ Circle Tim's room on the map he made.

In the Classroom

Tim knows the location of all the things in his classroom. Tim and his classmates are drawing a map of these places.

2 Look at the classroom map. Draw a box around the location of the reading area.

At School

Tim knows all the important places in his school. He even has a map of his school. The map of Tim's school has symbols. Symbols are pictures that stand for real things. The map key tells what the symbols mean.

TextWork

3 Circle the rooms that are next to the cafeteria on the school map.

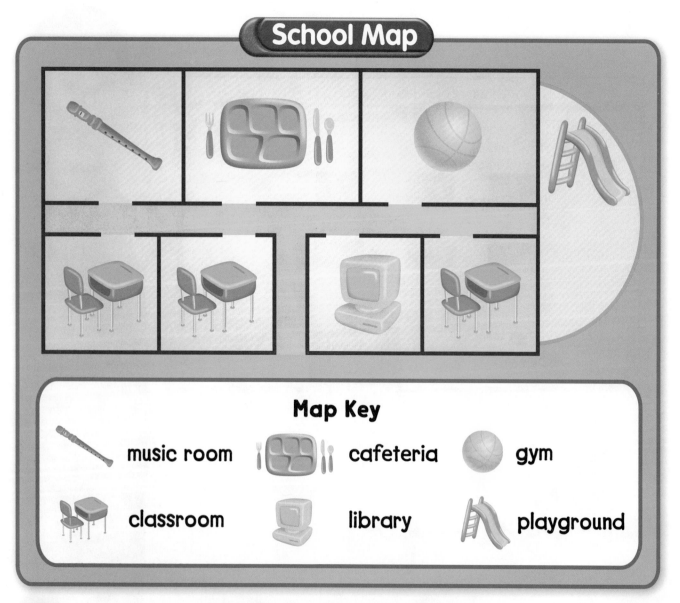

School Map

Map Key

music room   cafeteria   gym

classroom   library   playground

Making a Model

Tim used the map of his classroom to make a model of his classroom. Pictures and maps are flat. You can look at a model from all sides. When you look down on it, it is like a map.

TextWork

4 What flat items can be used to show a classroom?

_____

_____

5 Underline the way a map is different from a model.

121

① **SUMMARIZE** What can maps and models show about places?

_____

_____

② Tell about the **location** of a place in your school.

_____

_____

_____

③ When might you need to use a map?

_____

_____

_____

Activity

Make a map of your classroom. It should help new classmates find their way around. Show all the important places.

Finding Where You Are

A map can help us find our way around our neighborhood and community. A **neighborhood** is a part of a city or a town. A map can show our homes and other places. **How do you think this lesson will help you tell where you live?**

_____

_____

You can use a map to show where you live.

NORTH CAROLINA STANDARD COURSE OF STUDY

5.02 Investigate key features of maps.

5.03 Use geographic terminology and tools to create representations of the earth's physical and human features through simple maps, models, and pictures.

Your State

Maps can show many kinds of places. One map may show streets in a community. Another may show communities in a state. A **state** is a part of a country. North Carolina is a state. High Point is a community in North Carolina.

TextWork

❶ Look at the map. Find Greenville and circle it.

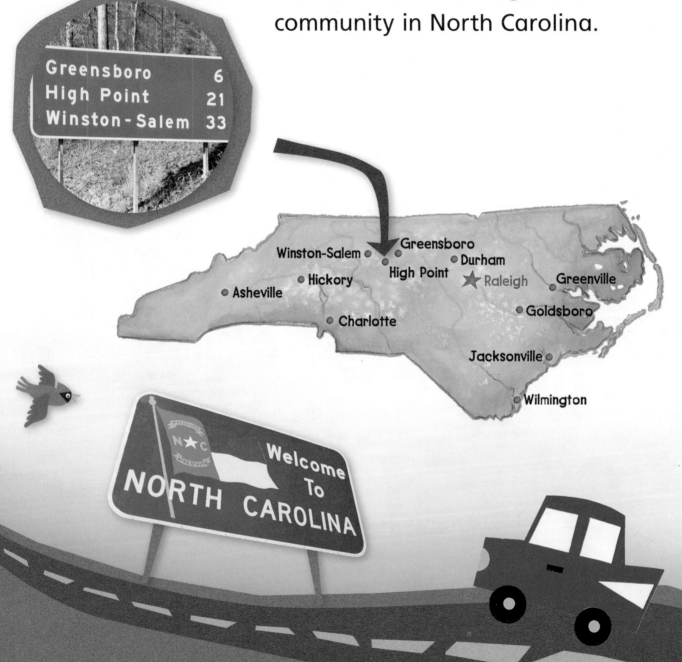

Greensboro   6
High Point   21
Winston-Salem   33

Winston-Salem   Greensboro
Durham
High Point
Hickory   ★ Raleigh   Greenville
Asheville
Goldsboro
Charlotte
Jacksonville
Wilmington

Welcome To NORTH CAROLINA

Your Country

Some maps show states and countries. A country is a land that has its own people and laws. The United States of America is our country. It has 50 states. North Carolina is one of these states.

Lines on a map show borders. A **border** is where a state or a country ends.

TextWork

❷ Look at the map. Draw a circle around North Carolina.

The United States

CANADA

ALASKA

WASHINGTON

MONTANA

NORTH DAKOTA

MINNESOTA

NEW HAMPSHIRE
VERMONT
MAINE

OREGON

IDAHO

SOUTH DAKOTA

WISCONSIN

MICHIGAN

NEW YORK

MASSACHUSETTS
RHODE ISLAND

WYOMING

NEVADA

NEBRASKA

IOWA

PENNSYLVANIA

CONNECTICUT
NEW JERSEY

UTAH

COLORADO

INDIANA OHIO
ILLINOIS

WEST VIRGINIA

DELAWARE
MARYLAND

CALIFORNIA

KANSAS

MISSOURI

KENTUCKY

VIRGINIA

Washington, D.C.

PACIFIC OCEAN

ARIZONA

NEW MEXICO

OKLAHOMA

TENNESSEE

NORTH CAROLINA

ARKANSAS

ALABAMA

SOUTH CAROLINA

TEXAS

MISSISSIPPI

GEORGIA

ATLANTIC OCEAN

LOUISIANA

FLORIDA

HAWAII

MEXICO

Gulf of Mexico

Your Continent

Some maps show countries and continents. A **continent** is a very large area of land. There are seven continents on Earth. They are North America, South America, Europe, Africa, Asia, Australia, and Antarctica. The United States is on the continent of North America.

TextWork

3 Look at the map. Find the United States. Draw a circle around it.

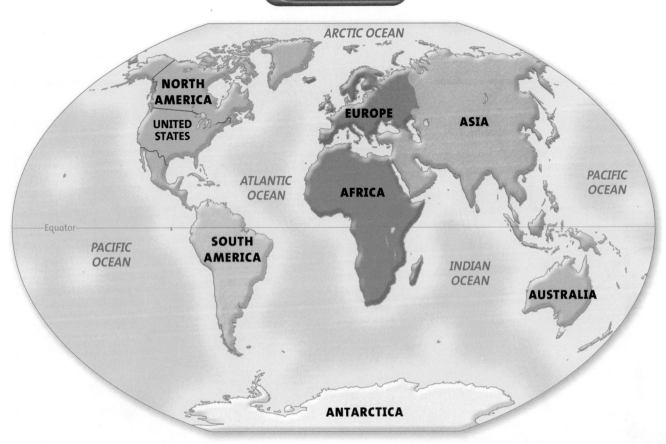

The World

ARCTIC OCEAN

NORTH AMERICA

UNITED STATES

EUROPE

ASIA

ATLANTIC OCEAN

AFRICA

PACIFIC OCEAN

Equator

PACIFIC OCEAN

SOUTH AMERICA

INDIAN OCEAN

AUSTRALIA

ANTARCTICA

Colors on a Map

Most maps use colors to show land and water. Different colors show land. Blue shows water. Rivers are blue lines on a map. Sometimes a river is a border of a state or a country.

TextWork

4 What color on a map shows water?

_____

North Carolina

Elizabeth City
Greensboro
Winston-Salem
•Durham
Chapel Hill
★Raleigh Greenville
Asheville• Hickory
•Charlotte
•Fayetteville
Jacksonville•
•Wilmington

ATLANTIC OCEAN

A globe is a model of Earth. A globe also uses colors to show land and water.

1 SUMMARIZE How can a map help you tell where you live?

_____

_____

_____

2 How are a **state** and a country different?

_____

_____

3 How can you tell where land and water are on a map?

_____

_____

_____

Writing

✏ Look at a map. Write sentences that tell where you live.

Land and Water

Different parts of the United States have different kinds of land. Some communities are on land that is high. Some are on land that is low. Many communities are near water. **What do you think you will learn about land and water?**

_____

_____

The Great Smoky Mountains

**NORTH CAROLINA
STANDARD COURSE OF STUDY**

5.06 Compare and contrast geographic features of places within various communities.

5.07 Explore physical features of continents and major bodies of water.

129

① Underline the mountains that are in North Carolina.

Mountains and Hills

Some communities are near mountains. A **mountain** is the highest kind of land. The Blue Ridge Mountains are in North Carolina. So are the Great Smoky Mountains.

Other communities are near hills. A **hill** is land that rises above the land around it. There are many hills in North Carolina.

mountain

hills

Valleys and Plains

Some people live in valleys. A **valley** is low land that is between mountains. Maggie Valley is in North Carolina. It is between some of the Great Smoky Mountains.

Other people live on plains. A **plain** is land that is mostly flat. The land in plains is good for growing food. North Carolina has many plains.

2 What kind of land is good for growing food?

_____

valley

plain

131

Lakes and Rivers

Many people live near water. Some live near lakes. Lakes can be big. Lakes can be small.

Other people live near rivers. People can use rivers to go places by boat.

lake

river

Oceans

The water in rivers moves across the land to the ocean. An **ocean** is a large body of water. The land near an ocean is mostly flat. The Atlantic Ocean and the Pacific Ocean are borders of the United States. Many people live near these oceans. North Carolina is next to the Atlantic Ocean.

TextWork

④ Name one ocean that is next to the United States.

_____

_____

ocean

1 SUMMARIZE What kinds of land and water does North Carolina have?

_____

_____

_____

2 How are a **mountain** and a **valley** different?

_____

_____

_____

3 What are three kinds of land?

_____

_____

_____

Activity

Make a chart showing the kinds of land and water in North Carolina.

Communities can be different sizes. A town may be small. A **city** is a very large community. Cities have many people, many stores, and many streets. **What do you think you will learn about communities?**

_____

_____

Ron and his father live in the city of Raleigh, North Carolina.

**NORTH CAROLINA
STANDARD COURSE OF STUDY**

5.04 Analyze patterns of movement within the community.

Living in the Suburbs

TextWork

❶ What do we call a smaller community that is near a large city?

_____

Kyle lives in Wake Forest. Wake Forest is a suburb of Raleigh, North Carolina. A **suburb** is a smaller community near a large city. It has fewer people, stores, and streets than a city does.

Kyle's family moved to Wake Forest from Raleigh. It is quieter in Wake Forest than in Raleigh. There is less traffic. The homes have bigger yards.

Living in the Countryside

Some communities are far from cities and suburbs. They are in the countryside. People in these communities often live on farms. A **farm** is a place for growing plants and raising animals.

Sara lives on a strawberry farm in North Carolina. The strawberries grown on her family's farm are sold in North Carolina's cities and suburbs. They are brought on trucks to larger communities.

TextWork

❷ Underline the kind of farm Sara lives on.

1 **SUMMARIZE** What kinds of communities did you read about in this lesson?

_____

_____

2 What is the difference between a **city** and a **suburb**?

_____

_____

_____

3 Why might someone living in a city move to a suburb?

_____

_____

_____

Writing

Write about what it might be like to live on a farm.

Soil, trees, and water are some of Earth's resources. A **resource** is anything that people can use. People often live near resources. **What do you think you will learn about how people use resources?**

_____

_____

NORTH CAROLINA STANDARD COURSE OF STUDY

5.05 Demonstrate responsibility for the care and management of the environment within the school and community.

Taking Care of Earth

It is our responsibility to take care of Earth's resources. We can keep the land and water clean. We can plant trees to take the place of trees people have cut down.

Planting trees is one way to care for resources in your community.

Children in History

Conrad Reed

In 1799, 12-year-old Conrad Reed found a lump of gold in Cabarrus County, North Carolina. Gold is a resource. After his find, many people came to North Carolina to look for more gold. This was the first gold rush in the United States.

People can **recycle** old things to make new things. Plastic, paper, metal, and glass can be used again. People can reduce, or lower, the amount of resources they use. They can reuse things, or use them again.

We can do these things at school, too. We can reduce, reuse, and recycle to help save Earth's resources.

 TextWork

❶ Look at the pictures on page 140. Circle the resource that is being planted.

❷ Name one thing that you can recycle.

_____

Use bins like these to recycle things in your community.

RECYCLE AREA
PLEASE DEPOSIT RECYCLABLES ONLY

1 **SUMMARIZE** Why is it important for people to take care of Earth's resources?

_____

_____

_____

2 What are some ways you can **recycle** in your home?

_____

_____

3 What are some ways you can help take care of the community?

_____

_____

_____

Activity

Make a poster to show people in your school what they can recycle.

Review and Test Prep

 The Big Idea

People live in many different places. We can tell about where we live by using maps and globes.

Summarize the Unit

Focus Skill **Categorize and Classify** Fill in the chart. Show what you know about different places to live.

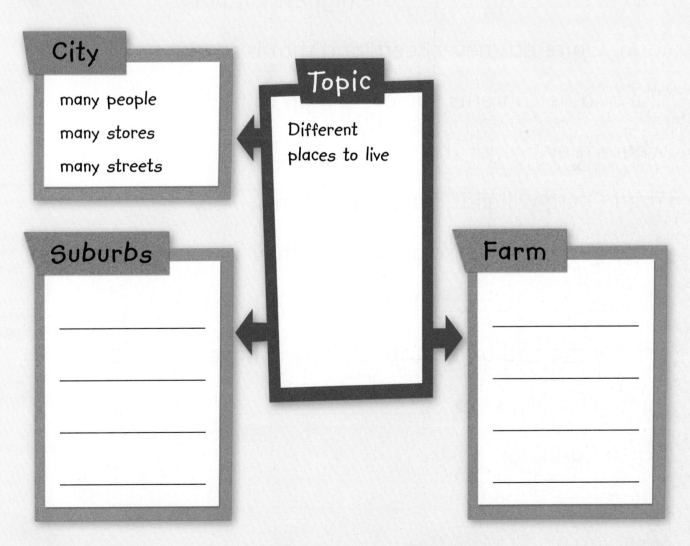

City

many people

many stores

many streets

Topic

Different places to live

Suburbs

_____

_____

_____

Farm

_____

_____

_____

143

Use Vocabulary

Fill in the blanks with the correct words.

Claire lives in a small community outside

of Charlotte, North Carolina. This kind of

community is called a ❶ _____.

Claire and her parents are going on a

camping trip. They are visiting a park with

a ❷ _____, the highest kind of

land. Claire has never seen land that is so high!

She and her parents will use a map to find

where they are, or their ❸ _____.

Then Claire will visit her grandparents. They

grow plants and raise animals on their

❹ _____. It is far away from the

city. By the end of her trip, Claire will have

been all over the ❺ _____ of

North Carolina.

Word Bank

location
  p. 117
state
  p. 124
mountain
  p. 130
suburb
  p. 136
farm
  p. 137

Think About It

Circle the letter of the correct answer.

6 Which color is used to show water on maps?
- **A** brown
- **B** green
- **C** red
- **D** blue

7 Which of these is a kind of high land?
- **A** plain
- **B** valley
- **C** hill
- **D** river

8 Which is something you would find on a farm?
- **A** many tall buildings
- **B** many animals
- **C** many stores
- **D** many people

9 Which resource can people plant?
- **A** trees
- **B** gold
- **C** rocks
- **D** water

Answer each question in a complete sentence.

10 Why are maps important?

_____

_____

11 What kinds of land and water do people live near?

_____

_____

Show What You Know

Writing Write a Letter
What words could you use to tell a pen pal about where you live? Write a short letter to your pen pal, telling about where you live.

Activity Make a Mural
With your class, create a mural to show where you live. Draw things in your community on the mural. Share your mural with another class.

GO online To play a game that reviews the unit, join Eco in the North Carolina Adventures online or on CD.

The Marketplace

A mother and daughter buy things in a grocery store.

Spotlight on Goals and Objectives

North Carolina Interactive Presentations

NORTH CAROLINA STANDARD COURSE OF STUDY

COMPETENCY GOAL 6 The learner will apply basic economic concepts to home, school, and the community.

 # The Big Idea

How do people make choices about how to spend money?

People in a community buy things from one another. They need money to buy things. People do work to get money for their families. Families must make choices about how to spend their money.

Draw a place where you go to buy things. Show some things that the place sells.

Cause and Effect

Learn

■ A cause is an event or action that makes something happen.

■ What happens is the effect.

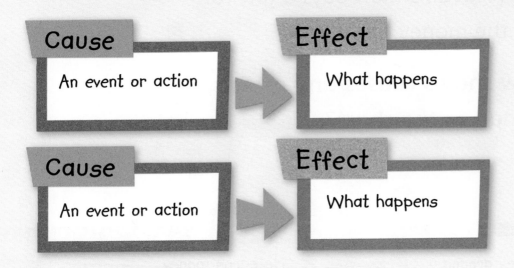

Cause

An event or action

→

Effect

What happens

Cause

An event or action

→

Effect

What happens

Practice

Read the paragraph below. Underline the effect of Carol's saving money.

Carol does chores every weekend. She earns money. Carol has saved a lot of money, so now she can buy a bicycle.

Cause

Effect

149

Apply

Read the paragraph.

Simon wants to buy his mother a gift for her birthday. He earns money for doing chores around the house. He keeps his money in a jar so that it does not get lost. Simon goes to the Gibsonville Fall Festival in Gibsonville, North Carolina. At the festival, Simon buys a gift for his mother with the money he saved.

The chart below shows causes and effects. What can you add to the chart?

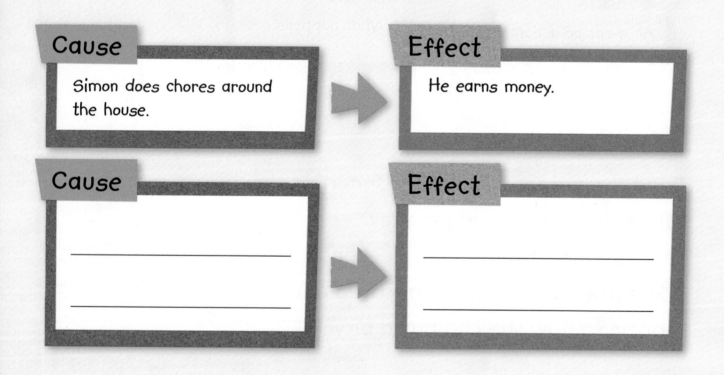

Cause	Effect
Simon does chores around the house.	He earns money.

Cause	Effect
_____	_____

Goods and Services

There are many kinds of workers. Some workers make goods. **Goods** are things that people make to sell. Some workers sell services. **Services** are the kinds of work people do for others. **What might you learn about working?**

_____

_____

Pet stores sell services and goods.

NORTH CAROLINA STANDARD COURSE OF STUDY

6.07 Recognize that all families produce and consume goods and services.

151

Workers Make Goods

TextWork

① Circle the goods in the pictures.

Some workers make goods. People can buy these goods in stores. Communities have many kinds of stores. These stores sell many kinds of goods.

Potter

Baker

Carpenter

152

Workers Sell Services

Some workers sell services. Services are the kinds of work people do for others for money. **Money** is what people use to pay for goods and services. A place where people sell goods or services is a **business**.

Bus driver

Hair stylist

Services and Prices

Haircut..............................$10

Shampoo and cut.................$12

Shampoo, cut, and style.......$16

TextWork

2 Circle the people in the pictures who are selling services.

153

③ Circle the producer in the picture.

Producers and Consumers

Some people work at making goods. Other people work at selling goods or services. All of these people are **producers**. People use money to buy goods and services. These people are **consumers**.

Consumers use money to buy fruits and vegetables.

Families Working

In your family, people work and buy goods and services. Families are made up of both producers and consumers. One or more of the people in your family may work. They use the money they earn to buy things for the family.

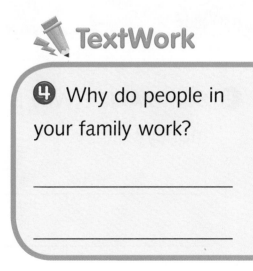
Your parents may drop you off at school on their way to work.

155

1 SUMMARIZE Why is it important to earn money?

_____

_____

2 How are **goods** and **services** the same?

_____

_____

How are they different?

_____

_____

3 Why does a community need both producers and consumers?

_____

_____

Writing

✏️ Write sentences about a good or a service that you would like to buy.

156

Things We Use

All people have needs. **Needs** are things we must have to live. People also have wants. **Wants** are things people would like to have. People earn money to buy things they want and need. **What will you learn about wants and needs?**

_____

_____

People shop for wants and needs.

NORTH CAROLINA STANDARD COURSE OF STUDY

6.01 Examine wants and needs and identify choices people make to satisfy wants and needs with limited resources.

6.02 Describe how people of different cultures work to earn income in order to satisfy wants and needs.

Things We Must Have

People need, or must have, food, clothing, and a place to live. Family members help one another meet their needs.

Family members share food with one another.

Things We Would Like

Families choose how to spend their money. They must first buy the things they need. Then they may use some of the money that is left for things they want. People can not buy everything they want. They must make choices.

Some things are scarce. When something is **scarce**, there is not much of it. It will cost more to buy.

TextWork

2 Nicholas loves to play soccer. Circle the picture of what he might choose to buy.

3 Circle the words for things that are needs.

Homes Around the World

Families all over the world have the same needs. They need food, clothing, and a place to live. Many families meet their needs in the same ways your family does. Some meet their needs in different ways.

Mongolia

Tanzania

Sweden

Jobs Around the World

Many people work at jobs. A **job** is work that a person does to earn money.

There are many kinds of jobs around the world. Some are like the jobs in your community. Some are different.

 **TextWork**

4 Underline the sentences that tell what kinds of jobs some people have.

Some people in Japan give music lessons.

Some people in Guatemala make cloth.

Some people in France work in restaurants.

1 **SUMMARIZE** How do people get the things they use every day?

_____

_____

_____

2 When is something **scarce**?

_____

_____

3 What are some kinds of jobs that people can have?

_____

_____

_____

Activity

Draw a picture of yourself doing a job that you might like to have one day.

Spending and Saving

Amy's community has a market. A **market** is a place where people buy and sell goods. Amy wants to spend some of her money. She also wants to save some. To **save** is to keep some money to use later. **What will you learn about spending and saving?**

_____

_____

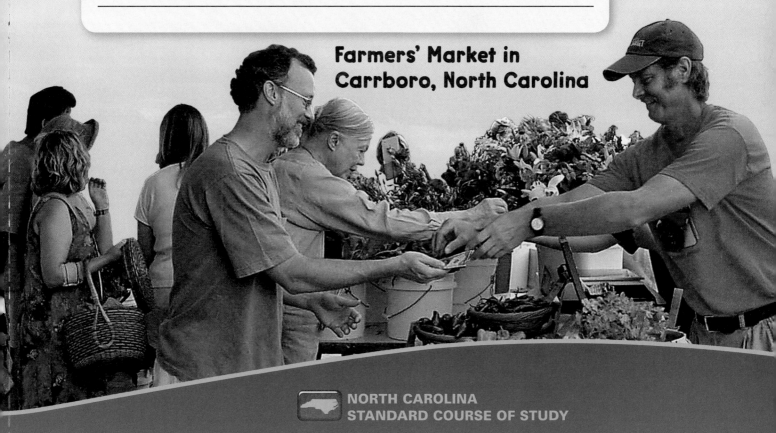

Farmers' Market in Carrboro, North Carolina

NORTH CAROLINA STANDARD COURSE OF STUDY

6.06 Identify the uses of money by individuals which include saving and spending.

Spending

Amy has money to spend at the market. She wants to buy a gift for her grandmother. Amy will think about things her grandmother likes. She will also think about how much money she has.

Buyers trade money for goods and services. When people **trade**, they give one thing to get another thing.

❶ At the market, is Amy a producer or a consumer? Circle your answer.

producer   consumer

Saving

Amy does not spend all of her money at once. She saves some of it to use later.

Many people put the money they save in a bank. A bank is a business that keeps money safe.

 **TextWork**

2 Underline the sentence that tells why people keep money in a bank.

1 **SUMMARIZE** Why do people spend some of their money and save some of it?

_____

_____

_____

2 What do people do at a **market**?

_____

_____

3 Why do people put their money in a bank?

_____

_____

_____

Writing

✏ Make a shopping list. Tell where you would go to buy the goods on your list.

Crayons are made in a factory. A **factory** is a building in which people use machines to make goods. Many people work at this crayon factory. In the factory, workers do different jobs. **What might you learn about factories?**

_____

_____

A crayon factory

**NORTH CAROLINA
STANDARD COURSE OF STUDY**

6.03 Participate in activities that demonstrate the division of labor.

How Crayons Are Made

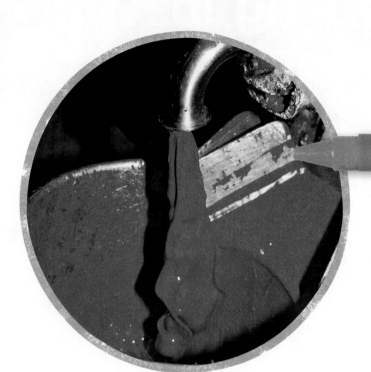

Step 1

Some factory workers mix hot, melted wax and colorings. The wax will give the crayons their shape. The colorings will give them their colors.

Step 2

TextWork

❶ What gives crayons their colors?

_____

_____

Other workers pour the hot, colored wax into molds. The molds shape the crayons.

Step 3

The molds are cooled with water. This helps the crayons get hard.

Step 4

More workers look at the crayons after they come out of the molds. These workers make sure that the crayons look right.

Step 5

In another part of the factory, a worker uses a machine to make colored labels. Another machine pastes the labels on the crayons.

Step 6

 TextWork

❸ Look at the pictures. Circle the picture that shows a machine making labels.

Workers put the crayons in boxes of different sizes. The boxes are then sent out to stores.

The crayons go to stores around the world. Your crayons went from the factory to a store near you. Then they came to your school.

4 Where do crayons go after they leave the factory?

_____

_____

Children in History

Addie Laird

Addie Laird was a young girl who worked in a factory long ago. At that time, many children had jobs in factories. They worked hard all day at unsafe machines. Children got hurt. People who saw this picture of Addie wanted to pass new laws. Now a child's job is to learn in school.

Lesson 4 Review

1 **SUMMARIZE** How are goods made in a factory?

_____

_____

_____

2 How is a **factory** different from a market?

_____

_____

_____

3 Why do factories need many workers?

_____

_____

_____

Activity

Draw a set of pictures that show how crayons are made. Show different workers doing each step.

Government Helps Us

Government workers clear snow from roads.

Government services are the things that a government does to make a community a good place to live in. Government workers help keep communities safe and clean. **What do you think you will learn about government services?**

_____

_____

NORTH CAROLINA STANDARD COURSE OF STUDY

6.04 Explore community services that are provided by the government and other agencies.

6.05 Give examples of the relationship between the government and its people.

173

Government Workers

There are different kinds of government workers. Police officers make sure that people follow the laws. Firefighters help when there is a fire.

Schools are government services. Teachers help you learn. You go to school to learn how to be a good citizen in the community.

TextWork

1 Name one government worker in your community.

_____

_____

Some government workers build roads.

Park rangers make sure parks stay clean. They help visitors to the parks stay safe.

Libraries are government services, too. Librarians help you find books for school. They give you ideas for books to read for fun, too.

TextWork

2 Circle the people who are government workers.

1 **SUMMARIZE** How do government services help people?

_____

_____

_____

2 What is one **government service**?

_____

_____

3 How do librarians help you?

_____

_____

_____

Writing

✎ Write sentences about a government service that helps keep your community clean or safe.

Review and Test Prep

 The Big Idea

People trade goods and services with one another. They make choices about how to spend their money.

Summarize the Unit

(Focus Skill) Cause and Effect Fill in the chart. Show what you have learned about spending and saving money.

Cause

People work at jobs.

➡️

Effect

_____

_____

_____

Cause

_____

_____

_____

➡️

Effect

People use money they have saved to buy something they want.

Use Vocabulary

Write the word under its meaning.

1 a place where people buy and sell goods

_____

2 a building in which people use machines to make goods

_____

3 things people make or grow to sell

_____

4 work people do for others for money

_____

5 to give one thing to get another

_____

Think About It

Circle the letter of the correct answer.

6 Which of these is a service?

    A cutting hair

    B a book

    C a toy

    D a crayon

7 Which of these is a need?

    A books

    B food

    C games

    D toys

8 Where do people put their money to keep it safe?

    A a bank

    B a market

    C a factory

    D a business

9 Which of these jobs is a government service?

    A dog walker

    B hair stylist

    C librarian

    D store clerk

Answer each question in a complete sentence.

10 Why do people work at jobs?

_____

_____

11 Why is it important for people to save some of their money?

_____

_____

Show What You Know

Writing Write a Story
Think about how you use your money. Make up a story about someone choosing how to use his or her money.

Activity Make a Classroom Market
Each person should act out a different job people have in a market. Choose what you will sell. Draw goods or services and money. Sell the goods or services so you can buy more.

GO online To play a game that reviews the unit, join Eco in the North Carolina Adventures online or on CD.

180

Technology We Use Today

Students work in a computer lab.

Spotlight on Goals and Objectives

North Carolina Interactive Presentations

NORTH CAROLINA STANDARD COURSE OF STUDY

COMPETENCY GOAL 7 The learner will recognize how technology is used at home, school, and in the community.

The Big Idea

How does technology help connect communities?

Technology is all of the tools we use to make our lives easier. We use technology at home and in school. Communication and transportation connect us with communities all over the world.

Draw a picture of a kind of technology that you use.

Recall and Retell

Learn

■ To recall is to remember.

■ To retell is to tell about something in your own words.

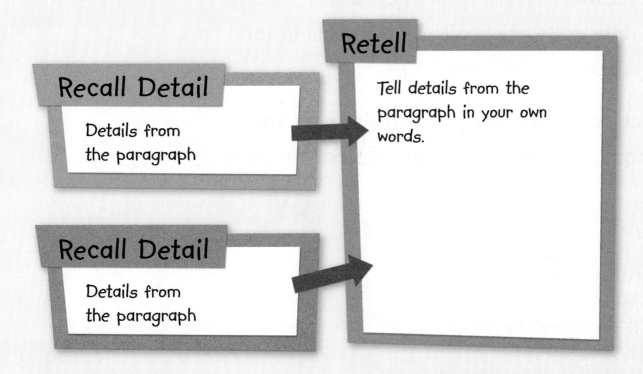

Retell

Tell details from the paragraph in your own words.

Recall Detail

Details from the paragraph

Recall Detail

Details from the paragraph

Practice

Read the paragraph below. Underline two details that you can use to retell the paragraph.

John uses the Internet for many things. He finds information. He sends e-mails to his pen pal in Japan. John also uses the Internet to play games.

Detail

Apply

Read the paragraph.

Ms. Jones is planning a trip to visit her brother in Raleigh, North Carolina. She uses the Internet to find information about airplane flights. She watches television to find out what the weather is like in North Carolina. Finally, Ms. Jones calls her brother on the telephone to tell him when she is coming.

The chart below recalls details from the paragraph. What can you add to the chart?

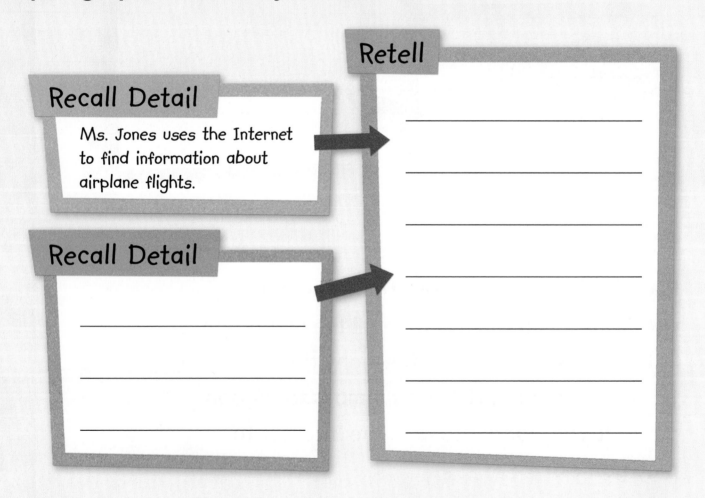

Retell

Recall Detail

Ms. Jones uses the Internet to find information about airplane flights.

Recall Detail

Communication

Every day, people talk or write to share their ideas and feelings. This sharing is called communication. We use communication at home, at school, and at play. **What might you learn about communication?**

_____

_____

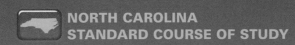

NORTH CAROLINA STANDARD COURSE OF STUDY

7.01 Compare and contrast the use of media and forms of communication at home and in other social environments.

Telephones

Long ago, people could only write letters to communicate with people far away. Letters took a long time to get where they were going. When telephones were made, people could communicate by talking. Now people can use cell phones to send pictures, music, videos, and e-mail.

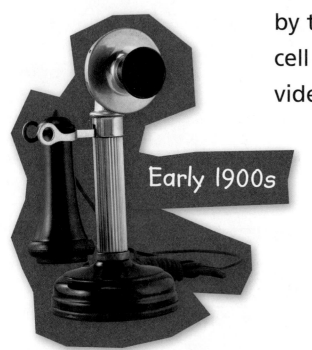

Early 1900s

1950s

Today

Computers and the Internet

Today, people can send letters and pictures by e-mail. E-mail uses the Internet. The **Internet** links computers around the world.

Many people now have computers in their homes. Some use laptop computers when they are away from home. Students can use computers in schools.

 **TextWork**

2 Circle the pictures of tools that you use every day.

Communication

Past | Present

In the past, computers were very large.

187

1 SUMMARIZE What are some ways to communicate?

_____

_____

_____

2 How do people use the **Internet**?

_____

_____

3 What are some ways communication was different in the past?

_____

_____

_____

Writing

Write sentences about the ways you communicate with others.

Connecting Communities

Elena lives in Charlotte, North Carolina. Her grandparents live in Rio de Janeiro, Brazil. They use communication and transportation to connect their communities. **What might you learn about technology and communities?**

_____

_____

Elena uses the computer to communicate.

**NORTH CAROLINA
STANDARD COURSE OF STUDY**

7.02 Describe how communication and transportation link communities.

189

Connecting with People

Elena communicates with her grandparents. She sends e-mails and talks on the telephone. Elena's family also uses transportation. They go by airplane to visit one another.

Charlotte

Atlantic Ocean

Pacific Ocean

Rio de Janeiro

Technology Connects Us

Technology has made communication easier. Television and the Internet connect us with people all over the world.

Technology has also made transportation easier. People go by car, bus, train, or airplane.

In the future, new technology will help connect us. The **future** is the time that has not yet come.

Biography
Cooperation

The Wright Brothers

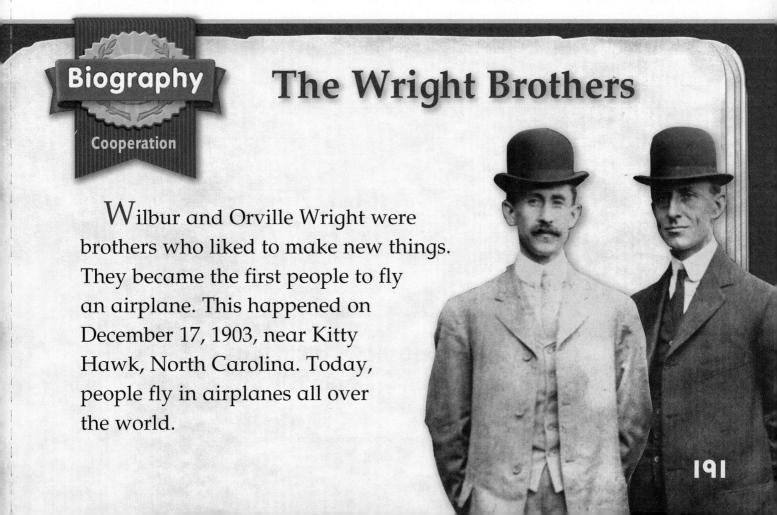

Wilbur and Orville Wright were brothers who liked to make new things. They became the first people to fly an airplane. This happened on December 17, 1903, near Kitty Hawk, North Carolina. Today, people fly in airplanes all over the world.

1 **SUMMARIZE** How does technology connect communities?

_____

_____

_____

2 Use the word **future** in a sentence.

_____

_____

3 What kinds of transportation can help you go to places far away?

_____

_____

_____

Activity

Draw a picture that shows a kind of transportation you think people will use in the future.

Using Technology

Technology makes it easier for people to learn and to share. You can use computer technology to find facts about many things. A **fact** is something that is true. It is not made up. **What might you learn about using technology?**

_____

_____

North Carolina has many mountains.

Children use technology in school.

NORTH CAROLINA STANDARD COURSE OF STUDY

7.03 Use the computer and other technological tools to gather, organize, and display data.

Technology Resources

Two technology resources you can use are the Internet and computer disks. Your school or community library may have CD-ROMs or DVDs. These have facts. You can also learn facts on television and radio.

TextWork

❶ Underline one place to find facts.

❷ Circle the resources that tell the latest news.

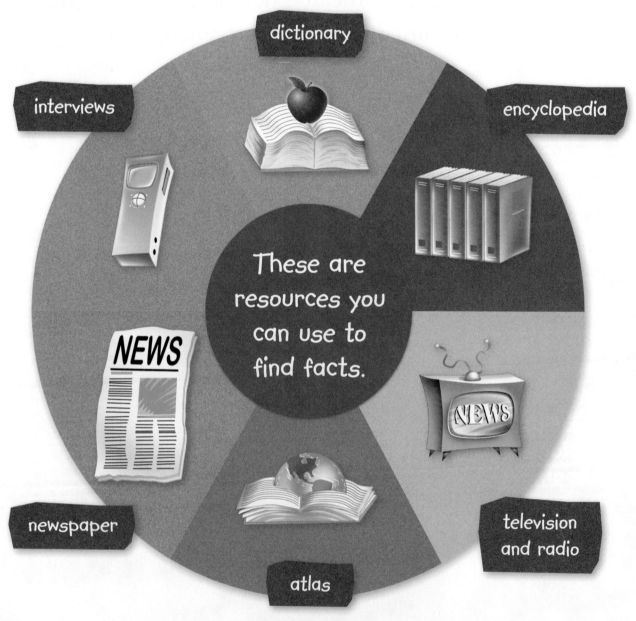

dictionary

interviews

encyclopedia

These are resources you can use to find facts.

NEWS

NEWS

newspaper

atlas

television and radio

Using the Internet

Use Internet sites you know you can trust. Use the Internet only with an adult you trust.

- Use a mouse and a keyboard to look for facts.

- Type in key words.

- Read carefully and take notes.

- Print a paper copy.

 **TextWork**

3 Who should always be with you when you are using the Internet?

_____

You can use computers to print out and show the information you find on the Internet.

1 **SUMMARIZE** What are some ways people can use technology to find facts?

_____

_____

2 Write one **fact** about technology resources that you learned from this lesson.

_____

_____

3 Retell in your own words some tips for finding facts on the Internet.

_____

_____

_____

Writing

Use technology resources you read about in this lesson. Find facts about something. Write about what you find out.

Review and Test Prep

The Big Idea

The technology we use today connects people and communities around the world.

Summarize the Unit

Recall and Retell Fill in the chart. Show what you have learned about technology. Then retell the information in your own words.

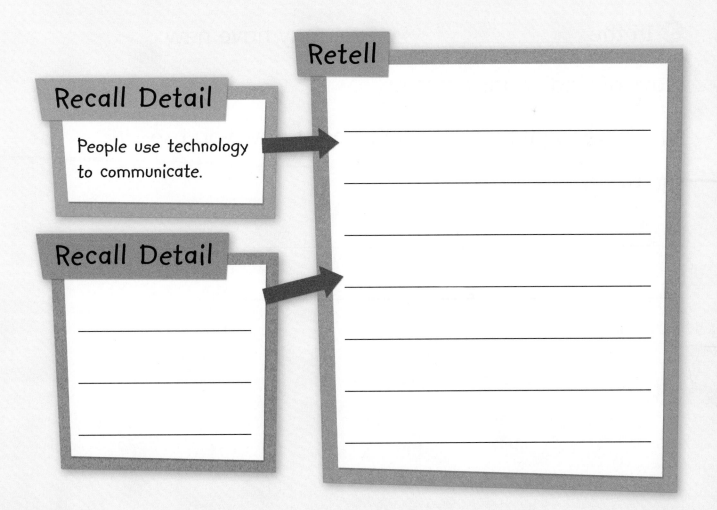

Retell

Recall Detail

People use technology to communicate.

Recall Detail

Use Vocabulary

Fill in the blanks with the correct words.

Word Bank

Internet
  p. 187
future
  p. 191
fact
  p. 193

1 We have many ways of finding a

_____, or information that is

true and not made up.

2 One way of finding information is by

using the _____, which links

computers around the world.

3 In the _____, we may have new

ways of finding information.

4 Write a sentence that tells about how you use

the **Internet**.

_____

_____

Think About It

Circle the letter of the correct answer.

5 Which is a kind of technology we use for communication?

    A car

    B horse and wagon

    C airplane

    D cell phone

6 Which is a kind of transportation we use to go to places far away?

    A walking

    B horse and wagon

    C airplane

    D bicycle

7 Which is a kind of technology we can use to find information?

    A train

    B airplane

    C car

    D computer

8 Which is one of the steps for finding facts on the Internet?

    A Type in key words.

    B Call a friend.

    C Read a book.

    D Play a game.

Answer each question in a complete sentence.

9 How can technology help you find information?

_____

_____

10 How has the Internet changed the way people communicate?

_____

_____

Show What You Know

Writing Write a Paragraph
What kinds of technology might we have in the future? Write about a new kind of technology for the future.

Activity Make an Internet Safety Poster
List safety rules for using the Internet. Make a poster showing the rules.

GO online To play a game that reviews the unit, join Eco in the North Carolina Adventures online or on CD.

For Your Reference

GLOSSARY

INDEX

R1

Glossary

The Glossary has important words and their definitions. They are listed in alphabetical (ABC) order. The definition is the meaning of the word. The page number at the end tells you where the word is first defined.

B

ballot
A list that shows all the choices people can vote for. p. 46

border
The place where a state or country ends. pp. 18, 125

business
A place where people sell goods or services. p. 153

C

cardinal directions
The directions of north, south, east, and west. p. 19

celebration
A time to be happy about something special. p. 91

change
To become different. p. 58

citizen
A person who lives in and belongs to a community. p. 29

city
A very large community. pp. 15, 135

communication
The sharing of ideas and feelings. p. 61

community
A group of people who live and work together. It is also the place where they live. p. 11

compass rose

The symbol on a map that shows directions. p. 19

consequence

Something that happens because of what a person does or does not do. p. 39

consumer

A person who buys goods and services. p. 154

continent

One of the seven main land areas on Earth. pp. 14, 126

country

An area of land with its own people and laws. pp. 15, 73

culture

A group's ways of life. p. 14

custom

A way of doing something. p. 14

fact

Something that is true and not made up. p. 193

factory

A building in which people use machines to make goods. p. 167

fair

Acting in a way that is right for all. p. 37

family

A group of people who live together. p. 5

farm

A place for growing plants and raising animals. p. 137

flag

A piece of cloth with symbols on it. p. 87

freedom

A kind of right. p. 42

GLOSSARY

future

The time that has not yet come. p. 191

 G

globe

A model of Earth. p. 14

goods

Things that people make or grow to sell. p. 151

government

A group of people who lead a community and make laws. p. 45

government service

A service that the government does for the community. p. 173

 H

hero

A person who does something to help others. p. 97

hill

Land that rises above the land around it. p. 130

history

The story of what happened in the past. p. 63

holiday

A day of celebration for everyone. p. 91

 I

immigrant

A person who comes from another place to live in a country. p. 18

inset map

A small map that is inside a larger map. p. 18

Internet

A system that links computers around the world. p. 187

job
Work that a person does to earn money. p. 161

landmark
A symbol that is a place people can visit. p. 103

law
A rule that people in a community must follow. p. 31

leader
A person who works to help a group. p. 33

location
The place where something is. p. 117

map
A flat drawing that shows where places are. p. 14

map key
The part of a map that shows what the symbols on the map mean. p. 19

map symbol
A small picture or shape on a map that stands for a real thing. p. 17

map title
The title of a map. pp. 17, 19

market
A place where people buy and sell goods. p. 163

mayor
The leader of a community. p. 35

money
What people use to pay for goods and services. p. 153

mountain
The highest kind of land. p. 130

N

national holiday
A day to remember a person or an event that is important to our country. p. 97

needs
Things we must have to live. p. 157

neighborhood
A part of a town or city. p. 123

O

ocean
A large body of water. pp. 14, 133

P

past
The time before now. p. 57

plain
Land that is mostly flat. p. 131

present
The time now. p. 57

principal
The leader of a school. p. 34

producer
A person who makes goods or sells goods and services. p. 154

R

recycle
To make something old into something new. p. 141

religion
A set of beliefs about God or gods. p. 92

resource
Anything that people can use. p. 139

respect
To treat someone or something well. p. 43

responsibility
Something that people should do. p. 41

right

Something people are free to do. p. 41

role

The part a person plays in a group or a community. p. 6

rule

Something that tells people how to act. p. 29

S

save

To keep something, such as money, to use later. p. 163

scarce

Not much of something. p. 159

services

Kinds of work people do for others for money. p. 151

settler

A person who makes a home in a new community. p. 104

share

To use something with others. p. 5

state

A part of a country. pp. 15, 124

suburb

A smaller community near a large city. p. 136

symbol

A picture that stands for an idea or a thing. p. 87

T

technology

All of the tools we use to make our lives easier. p. 67

tool

Something a person uses to do work. p. 67

trade

To give one thing to get another. p. 164

tradition

Something that is passed on from older family members to children. p. 15

transportation

Any way of moving people and things. p. 70

valley

Low land between mountains. p. 131

volunteer

A person who works without pay to help people. p. 43

vote

A choice that gets counted. p. 45

wants

Things we would like to have. p. 157

world

All the people and places on Earth. p. 17

Index

The index tells where information about people, places, and events in this book can be found. The entries are listed in alphabetical order. Each entry tells the page or pages where you can find the topic.

INDEX

INDEX
